SOCIAL CHANGE HOW INFLUENCES ORGANIZATIONAL

REWARD PLAN CHANGES

JOHN LOK

Contents

Preface

Introduction

How social change influences human behavioral change ? Why human behavior may be influenced by social change? Our individual behavior whether can be influenced to bring negative or positive attitude by social change? I shall attempt to indicate cases to explain whether our individual behavior can be influenced to changed by social environment change. Readers can have more understand how and why social change may influence our behavior in possible. Behavioral economy is one useful and fun social subject. Behavioral economists ususally research how and why human behaviors may influence economy growth or recession, or how and why economy environment changing factor may influence human behavior changes. This book research how social change influences organizational reward plan behavioral changes.

In my this book, I shall attempt to explain how and why ecommerce may be one kind network human job. Also, I shall indicate reasons to explain why human network behavior may bring direct or indirect influences to economy growth or recession in our global societies in macro and micro economy view. Why leisure changing environment may influence human behavior , even economic environment changes. I shall indicate cases to explain any possible human social activities may bring direct or indirect influences to cause our social economic growth or recession in consequency in possible as well as hoq any why social change influences organizational reward behavioral plan changes. I hope that my readers can feel more understanding whether what real meaning of behavioral economy is the relationship between our behaviors and our economy and organizational reward plan changes.

Contents

PROLOGUE

Contents

I

How social change influences organizational reward plan behavioral changes

The relationship between social change and organizational reward plan implement

Reward strategy can be applied to large organization, it can be also applied to small organization, e.g. family business, family business also needs compensation policies, the result encourages professional growth among family members and other employees as well as strategic business goal accomplishment. In general, compensation can be divided into the categories of base pay (equity as a basic for fairness , benefit, e.g. health care insurance, salry , wages, incentive compensation (e.g. bonuses, deferred compensation, stock or share options) and perks e.g. club membership, use of the company's private mountain, beach for holiday entertainment or sport activities e.g. free glof sport and company 's automobiles to provide to employees to drive in their private time.

Craig, E. A (2011) indicated that although small business has less employees , but it also needs compensatin adjustments. The reasons include: (1) performance-based increases i.e. a rise, (2) annual wage adjustments e.g. cost of living increases to remain with what comparable businesses are paying and corrective adjustments to more pay for a position into with other position in the business increases are considered to be a key component of compensation by managers and non-management employers alike. The difference between one small organization's and one large organization's performance based incresae is possible that one large organization has more a rise amount of performance -based increases in every time performance review. Otherwise, one small organization has less a rise amount of performance -based increases in every time performance review. A good reward strategy can develop a philosophy of compensation that builds a framework for base pay and incentive tailored to the special values, goals, and needs of the particular family firm. Hence, one family or small firm's compensation -reward strategy can be explained to be needed, due to these factors : the firm can compare pay and performance levels with those of businesses with whom which compete for employees, the firm's goal is to provide total compensation between median and the percentage of comparble groups, base salary will be made more accurate decision at or high or below the median level for the comparable groups, individual salaries will be made more accurate decision within how much percent of the midpoint for the firm's comparison group's salary range, the firm can make more accurate decision on emphasizing whether performance -based incentives ought be spent at the expense of the salary, whether annual incentives ought be exceed those of comparably sized competitors, whether long-term incentives ought be based on results that add shareholder value. However, culture can influence some business owners how to make compensation issues, culture means beliefs, values, assumption, habits and behavior patterns of the organization. The reasons staffs are paid the way, they are may be partly unconscious and may arise from the personal and family history and the deeply felt personal needs of the business leader or leaders. So, any family or small business will ought try to develop a philosophy of compensation (reward) strategy , which may learn a great deal about itself in the process. For example, a entrepreneur has confidence in her or his ability to manage compensation on a case-by-case basis and maintain tight personal tight personal control over each individual pay, perks, incentives, dividends, and gifts in order to encourage its employees can raise more effort to increase the sale number to its different kinds of product in its shop. Otherwise, if a family member working in this kind of culture asks for a raise, the business owner will not talk to about how to raise compensation to his/her salespeople in christmas period. Hence , culture seems to influence the large organization and small organization how to make itself compensation to salepeople in christmas period.

However, a basis for fairness to base pay which can let the large organization or small organizaion's staffs to feel, it is very important , when the large or small organization needs to focus on filling a vacancy and getting new skills into key areas quickly to meet customer needs with quality and efficiency. Because if the large organization or small organization expects it sale turnover may increase or staff turnover may decrease, but hiring needed talent may become more difficult, indicating that the company's pay structure may have lost internal logic if it's basic pay is unfair to attract talent staffs choose to join to its organization to work, when they feel that the organization's base pay is not reasonable to compare its competitors (pay for one job compared to another), and comparable jobs outide the company, the process is logical , objective and fair to be needed to judge the base pay structure to any organizations. Having a consistent, explainable rationable for how compensation or reward is critical for employee and shareholders judgements about fairness. Hence, individual employee will usually compare his/her job in the company's salary and his/her similar job in another company's salary whether whose salary is same or more or less between whose's company salary and similar company salary. Hence, a company needs to establish equitable base pay in a market value and merit system, with any adjustments , pay raises being a function of performance merit in order to make more reasonable compensation or reward to let its staffs to feel to avoid staff turnover number raises.

A rational compensation system steps can include: creating job description for all jobs, conducting a job evaluation to rank order jobs and determining which jobs that are similar in their importance to the business, obtaining extermal wage and salary survey information for representation jobs, utilizing other sources for comparabl external data when needed, determining the company's reward strategy for compensation and deciding whether it wants pay to be set at the market average , whether it wants compensation at levels above or below the market average, or whther it wants to make a culture statement with pay levels, creating a wage and salary structure of starting pay levels, (minimums) and levels of pay for the most experienced workers (maximums). Analyzing current pay levels against the new structure pay levels against the new structure to determine which jobs are paid appropriately and which ones are not, considerering individual, unique jobs that may have qualitative more or less important than external market comparables might suggest, making pay adjustments for those that are not of the range, accelerating regular increases for positions below the target range and decelerating or not making increased that are above the range. Finally , it needs to periodical check or review the wage and salary structure against outside benchmarket (external similar competitors positions to maintain external equity).

The point factor job evaluation tool can help the organization to make decision whether the staff ought pay how much salary level is the most reasonable. The point method include the elements such as : The experience element means the factor appraises the length of time normally required for an individual to acquire the necessary knowledge and ability to affectively perform the duties of the job. The experience level element means that whether the worker individual working experience in the firm, e.g. up to three months, he/she can earn the lowest points, till to comprehensive over right years, he/she can earn the highest points. The direction of others element means this factor appraises the responsibility to the job , it includes for organization, selection , assignment , guidance and review of personnel and the performance of other supervisory tasks. The direction of others level can indicate the employee earns none points when whose jobs involves no responsibility or authority for the direction of others, till to the highest points when the employee can confirm to own administrative abiluty,whose job is responsible for general administrative or executive supervision of all or broad segment of company operations as well as he/she can establish general policies and procedures and formulates and applies broad plans of operations.

Compensation specialists can help the company to select representative jobs from a company and find good external comparisions. They will need to make adjustment. Some criteria for determining a jobs's market value can include position title and job description, industry, size of company, sales or revenue volume, cost of living, based on location etc. data to determine whether their company's salary level is accaptable or reasonable to a job's market value. They need to gather the data concerns the job's market value. This is helpful because the latest supply and demand factors can affect certain positions may not show up in surveys. They must need to gather similar industry's organization size, sale or revenue volume data, daily cost of living and transportation cost how to influence their employees' income and similar competitors' employees income in order to make more reasonable and accurate salary structure adjustment.

reference
Craig, E.A. & Stephen, L.M. & John, L.W. (2011) family business compensation:
New York, US, Palgrave Macmillan, p.35

Good employee benefits and services can help the organization by reducing potential employee discontent, satisfying their needs and discouraging labor unrest or raisinf labor turnover. Thus, with competitive benefit programmes , an organization can be more effective in recruitment and employee retention, thus reducing labour turnover.

Employee benefits may include legally required payments, such as workers compensation, long service pay or retirement payment, sickness allowance and end of year payment, bonus as well as optional welfare plans,such as life insurance, medical/hospital /dental coverage to self and family' education allowance, housing allowance, quarters, subsidised loans, retirement, pension plan, meal allowance, travelling allowance, paid time off, pay sick leave, other specal paid leave, five day week, paid annual leave and maternity leave.

Employee service mean the organizations can choose to provide various services ranging from work related to those satisfying personal or family needs, in order to encourage employees to work happily and stay with a particular organization. The service may include social functions or recreational activities, e.g. New Year dinner, annual ball, company picnics, free transportation service, food service or canteen ,purchase of used equipment no longer required by the company, credit unions, low-interest loans, legal services, child care and elder care, conselling services, free holiday appartment, air ticket allowance etc. employees' welfares.

Strategy reward system pay for perform two elements: Financial reward includes base salary, pay incentives, employee benefits. Non-financial reward includes intrinsic rewards, centers in the work itself, praise, recognition , time off. Reward system is a key driver of-HR strategy, business strategy organization culture strategic reward system related to HR system. Such as skill-based pay to training, overtime pay rules to labor relations, sign-on bonus to employment, merit pay to performance management and merit pay to performance culture.

Every human being relationship blooms in the light of reward. As the world is going through a serious phase of recession, the amount which is paid to the employees and the form of payment done is therefore the issue that matters. The importance of Rewards is increasing in the world of commercial organisation and is definitely one of the major indicators of profitability and competitive advantages.

One of the biggest determinants of rewards lies in the financial position of a particular organisation. The organisations are in constant pressure of producing reward schemes which accumulate all the factors from attraction to motivation of their employees, simultaneously while maintaining the viability of the company's financial and commercial scenario. Absence of reward schemes may have a devastating effect on the organisations performance.

The concept of Total Reward has been evolving ever since, Management today is trying to widen up the meaning of the word 'Reward' including both tangible and intangible aspects of rewarding their employees, (Armstrong and Brown,1999). On one side the tangible rewards ensure financial stability of the employee while on the other side the intangible rewards looks after the employees luxuries and compensates for future loss. Now a day's managers and scholars are using Total Reward Management more and more as the modern management method

According to the Human resources management Total Reward strategy needs to b examined and experienced often to obtain perfect and efficient results. This strategy guarantees a remarkable profit for the organization improving the staff's performance as well as contains the potential to solve and compensate the existing issues in the organization. Rewarding employees in any organization can affect attitudes, behaviour and motivation. Influence on the behaviour of workers seems to be particularly important, it will tend to extra effort if an employee knows that his achievements, work, creativity etc. will be measured, evaluated and rewarded accordingly. The increasing efforts of the employees will result into the company's increasing profitability and better customer service. It must mobilize the growing individual and collaborative involvement of all employees.

Literature review:

Today organizations are looking forward to increase their employee's efforts by encouraging them to improve their performance beyond the organisations expectations and reducing labour cost to a minimum. Thus the study of employee motivation has constantly remained a managerial concern. This essay considers some of the main views of the organisations adopting a total reward approach to reward management. While answering such questions as what do you mean by total reward? How it is benefits the employees as well as the company? How does it motivate the employees? How is it monetarily profitable for the company? Etc.

"Reward management is concerned with the formulation and implementation of strategies and policies that aim to reward people fairly, equitably and consistently in accordance with their value to the organisation. It deals with the design, implementation and maintenance of reward processes and practices that are geared to the improvement of organizational, team and individual performance" (Armstrong and Murlis 2006). If the organisation has a fairly distributed reward management then it not only progresses the company but also enhances employee's skills and performance. Hence the organisation is under tremendous pressure of having a non bias reward distribution so as to avoid any chaos within the organisation.

"The reward management literature emphasizes the need to shift from short-term, ad hoc approaches to pay management to a longer-term, strategic approach. Changes in pay and benefits systems have therefore been prescribed as key HRM objectives, pulled together in the US literature under the rubric of the "new pay"" (Lawler, 1995)

It is therefore a major managerial concern about how they approach to the concept of total reward. Each organisation can have different criteria about elements that constitute total rewards.

Paul Thompson (2001), further gives an elaborated definition of total reward by emphasises it not only encompasses rational scientific elements like wages, changeable pay and profits, but also more intangible non money related elements such as scope to attain and implement responsibility, career opportunity, education and development, the inherent motivation delivered by the work itself and the quality of working life provided by the organization.

Essentially, the notion of total reward says that there is more to rewarding people than throwing money at them. Planning a long term reward holds the employee and motivates them to enhance their performance for better customer satisfaction. As Murlis and Watson (2001) refer to the importance of monetary values in designing a reward package but also about these not being the sole factors. She describes cash as being a weak tactic in the overall reward strategy and stresses that total reward policy should be based on building a much better understanding of what the employees expect in their rewards packages. Relationship between the organisation and the employees can be strengthened with the total reward approach.

Therefore we need to see a very integrated and holistic approach while considering all aspects of rewards (Armstrong and Murlis, 2006)

Hence it is essential to have a coherent reward strategy which "helps to create a work experience that meets the needs of employees and encourages them to contribute extra effort, by developing a deal that addresses a broad range of issues and by spending reward dollars where they will be most effective in addressing workers' shifting values.' O'Neal (1998).

CIPD reward faculty members Wright and Murlis have created a significant diagram to present visually the various types of total reward. Its definition incorporates a wide range of approach but it is not the only solution for employee energetic. The idea of reward exchange is emphasized although quite frequently left out in the area at work definition. In combination unique and common motivation methods are provided to employees in exchange accordingly for their effort, results, work time, creativity, talent etc. There are five main key elements to keep secure and retain talented workers and also to motivate them optimally to accomplish possibly best business results (Davis, 2007:4).

The key points stated by CIPD (2005) in the world at works total rewards: Compensation, Benefits, Work life, Performance, Development and career opportunities.

Manas and Graham (2003) emphasize that developing and implementing a total reward approach has much in common with reward strategy development. According to Purcell (2004) and colleagues 'the organisation can contribute by communicating the values, giving employees a voice, setting up improved performance management processes, instituting formal recognition schemes and taking steps to improve work/life balance'. Decisions such as giving voice to the employees by an organisation leads to the delegation of some powers to them regarding their respective expectation about rewards which helps the management in developing appropriate strategies.

Developing and implementing a total reward approach may be difficult but the benefits are considerable. The employment relationship created by a total reward approach, which makes the maximum use of relational as well as transactional rewards, will appeal more to and engage individuals involving people in their own reward package design, dives them strong messages about the organisation and its values. At its best, it builds relationship capital.

Pfeffer (1998) implicated a new idea to total reward approach in a powerful manner, Employees are able to use their skills in an effective and efficient way with interest and motivation in an enjoyable, challenging and empowered work environment, for which they should be shown appropriate appreciation by the organisation. This scenario creates such an environment for the employees, by which they got motivated and enhance their performance thereby proving beneficial for the company, but it would be less time consuming and simple to reward the employees monetarily then to plan and arrange intangible rewards.

Case Study:

Total Reward Statement as a document is created annually for every working member of the company on a regular basis. This document allows the employees to receive all the details regarding their benefits that have been received over the course of the year. As total rewards deals with tangible and non-tangible benefits it informs the employees about the salary drawn by them as well as a breakdown of all the other non-tangible profits that have been taken in exchange for their employment.

Presenting the reward to the employee in cash terms proves to be very beneficial for the company as well as the employee. For example: if an employee has received shares. The reward statement shows the value of the shares and might as well show their trading history since the issue of the previous statement.

There are many companies which have been adopting total reward strategies in the last few years and gaining benefits and improving their labour power. This paper shows a few companies dealing in different products and implementing total reward strategy.

Beginning with one of Europe's leading telecommunication services "BT COMMUNICATIONS". The new reward framework is one of the biggest change initiatives in BT's history, covering more than 40,000 employees in total.(e-reward.co.uk research report, no. 35, July 2005). The idea of transforming its reward strategy from fairly traditional multi-grade pay structure to a total reward system was BT's essential Organizational Program."One area of focus in the new strategic HR agenda was to look at reward and address BT's Paternalistic approach to reward" Says Kevin Brandy, HR Director Reward. (e-reward.co.uk, no. 35, July 2005).

As the management of BT states, the alleged reasons for switching from the previous reward arrangement was to develop the changed view of the BT people's regarding rewards. The organisation wasted Millions of pound annually on rewards because of the limitations of the employees in view of company's bonuses. Taking into consideration, the limitation of the earlier adopted reward strategy bounded employees to appreciate their benefits as well as lack understanding and awareness capabilities.

By implicating the new reward framework BT affect 250-plus market based roles in 18 job families. BT's strategy is basically based on the role and performance of the employees. As on the other hand, benefits and bonuses given are based on the external market. Giving total reward an broader offer BT has tried to renovate the reward strategy, by going beyond the standard remuneration of the base pay including bonuses.

For BT, total reward is not just an ordinary reward strategy used for paying wages to the employees. It's about bonus and benefits, such as company cars and health insurance, shares and pensions, role-based reward, performance-based pay and choice and flexibility in benefits provision. Henceforth three main elements of the reward package influence BT's new total reward approach: Base Salary, Bonus, Benefits (Armstrong and Thompson, 1999).

"STARBUCKS" being one of the world's largest speciality coffee retailer having 1300 store worldwide, hire around 200 people per day and grow US revenues by 25 to 30 percent on top of US$4.1 billion in revenues from the previous fiscal year. According to Chet Kuchinad, SVP of Total Pay "We build the Starbucks experience by delivering pay elements to our partners that drive financial rewards in the success of the company in a meaningful way." In order to strengthen and constrain the culture of Starbucks, innovative reward strategy and payment programs have been introduced. "Full- and part-time partners (who meet eligibility criteria) are offered health, dental, and vision insurance, as well as access to an employee assistance program (EAP), reimbursement accounts, short- and long-term disability, and Working Solutions, Inc. (a resource and referral service) to help manage work and family issues" (Wilson group.com, case study on Starbucks).The employees receiving the rewards greatly appreciate and value the reward and, as a result, provide a better a service to the customers.

According to Starbucks, total reward has played a very important role in benefitting the company but there are many other factors in human resources which affect the company's stability. Examples include employee education, an open n highly communicative environment and a unique program adopted by Starbucks called Mission Review, which is a part of a broader program called Partner Snapshot. Partner Snapshot deals with gaining feedback from the company's partners. However the functions of human resources in Starbucks continue. Rewards and profits were considered by the introduction of total reward that included additional health benefits, maturation of healthcare delivery, and coverage for same sex partners, and an employee assistance program.

"However, pay alone will not attract people. Our Total Pay philosophy and our culture of teamwork and community are all key parts of why people join and stay with Starbucks." (Starbucks)

The next case study deals with Audit, Consulting, Financial advisory, Risk management and Tax services. "DELOITTE" also known as Deloitte Touche Tohmatsu Limited (DDTL), is a UK private company limited by guarantee. Mark Carman, sales and marketing director of Motivano, Deloitte says "Total reward can b a win-win from the perspective of en employee as the reassurance and support available from knowing exactly what your salary and benefits package is worth can have a huge impact on their performance, engagement and motivation. With the rising value of rewards and benefits the company proprietor are using total reward to improve and support their affiliation with employees.

Deloitte explains five main steps in creating effective total reward communication:

Create clear and concise messages.

Think about brand and design.

Check the accuracy of your data.

Consider security of your personal information.

Work with other internal experts.

"BRISTOL-MYERS SQUIBB" is a US-owned pharmaceuticals company. Bristol-Mayers Squibb was going through a mystification of employees regarding reward strategies. As compared to the external competitive market the company was not able to reward the employees, employees were lacking the understanding of the reward which they received and there was an awareness that the wages and the benefits given to them were not as fine as the competitive market offered. Transformation to a flexible reward strategy was very necessary for Bristol-Mayers Squibb which supports the recruitment and maintenance, bringing all the strategies together Bristol introduced the total reward strategy.

Portraying everything as work experience, Bristol-Mayers Squibb kept the usual peculiarity between rewards and remuneration. As a result the company received employees which consists appreciation, work-life balance, civilization, employee development and the working environment

"HENNES & MAURITZ (H&M)" is a 100 billion SEK company, Engaged in designing and retailing of fashion apparel and accessories. Hennes & Mauritz appears to provide a total reward framework, with greater emphasis on relational rewards even though transactional rewards are provided (Armstrong (2006), pp.639-631). Hennes & Mauritz reward strategy includes many other human resources area like organizational traditions, conscription or selection etc. Implementing total reward management was a very successful concept in the history of Hennes & Mauritz. The increasing sales are the evidence of the profitability of H&M business as the employees are motivated with job satisfaction as a reward and perform their job as well as contribute their best to ensure customer satisfaction.

This case study acknowledges about the companies adopting total rewards from a long period of time and improving their business skills. Though there are some disadvantages to this approach. Starting with the employees, they find it very difficult to understand and expensive to set up as well as complicated to maintain. Although the advanced technology is helping organization to reduce burden as well as reduce cost. The vast range of choices may create a problem both to the company and the workers. There might also be wastage as the employees may not appreciate the full reward package.

Conclusion:

The reward approach not only takes care of the financial security of the employees but also looks after the overall development of their employees in the society. It's a delicate matter that should be perfectly balanced especially when the organization is rewarding different people working in one team. The advantages of total reward approach are substantial, but developing and putting it into practice may be a difficult task, by the use of relational and transactional rewards the employment relationships created by total rewards approach can be maximised. The total reward approach creates a strong communication about the organisation and its values by satisfying the employees and engaging them in their own designed reward package. At its best, it builds relationship capital

On conclusion, University HR strategic reward management system(review promote monitor scheme) aims to improve systems and skills for teaching employee communication, support teaching management to play a move active role in communicatin key messages, ensure school reward policies and procedures are fair to teaching staffs and administrative non-teacing staffs in salary rank increasing level, establish improved consultation procedures at academic and teaching service level, demonstrate the values and ethics by the university through management practices and communication with teaching staffs and non-teaching staffs, improve the profile and performance of the university by recruiting and developing talent teaching employees with appropriate external recognition , certain academic disciplines present more different recruitment challenges and profile of the university as an employer could be improved in the academic labour market, recruiting sample of selection decisions through early stages of employment to assess quality of appointment and identify learning points, suppoet and encourage recuritment messages to improve selection practive including skills and high quality appointment decisions, raise the profile of the university as an employer regionally, natinally and internationally, establish succession planning for all key roles and positions linked with clear career progression with job families, to face in a difficult economic climate the university needs to continue to attract and keep high quality staff to work in an efficient and cost effective manner. The extension of workload allocation models to all academic units is an important tool to assit in managing workload fairly and more effectively, well targeted and designed training and development is very effective in motivating and enabling staff and support productivity. Thus, social changing factor may influence how organization makes decision to implement reward plan.

II
How social change influences organization paying structure plan

How and why social change influences organizational paying structure plan Human professionals might create the pay structure for their organization, or they might work with an external compensation consultant. There are several steps to design a pay structure: job analysis, job evaluation, pay survey analysis, pay policy and development and pay structure information (Milkovish, G., & Newman, J. 2008).

Milkovich, G. & Newman, J. (2008) explaines that the pay structure steps include as below:

Step one : Job analysis is the process of studying jobs in an organization. The outcome of this process is a job description that includes the job title, a summary of the job tasks, asjust of the essential tasks and responsibilities and a description that includes the knowledge, skills and abilities needed to perform the job.

Step two: Job evaluation is the process of judging the relative worth of jobs in an organization. The outcome of job evaluation is the development of an internal structure or hierarchial ranking of jobs. Job-based evaluation is used more often than person-based evaluation and so the former will be the focus in this case. There are three methods of job-based evaluation: The point method, ranking and classification. The job evaluation helps to ensure that pay is internally worth perceived to be fair by employees.

Step three : Pay policy identification is the process of determining whether the organization wants to lead or meet the market in compensation. The pay policy or strategy will likely influence employee attraction. Pay policies can vary across families , i.e. groups of similiar jobs, and job level of the top management feels that different areas of the organization.

Step four: Pay survey analysis is the process of analysising compensation data gathered from other employers in a survey of the relevant labor market. Gathering enternal data , e.g. base pay, bonuses , stock or share options and benefits is the essential to kep the organization's compensation externally competitive within the industry. Employee attraction can be improved by maintaining externally pay structures.

Step five: Pay structure creation is the final step, in which the internal structure (step two of job evaluation) is combined with the external market pay rates . Step four: Pay survey analysis in a simple regression to develop a market pay line. Depending on whether the organization wants to lead or meet the market, the market pay line can be adjusted top or down. To complete the pay structure , pay grades and pay ranges are developed.

In this organization's job analysis, it can infleuce these positions or job titles. For example, office support department has the lower level, front line receptionist, middle level, admin. assistant and top level, assistant to the director of operatons. Operations department has the lower level, operations trainee, operations trainess, middle level , operations analyst, top level, director of regional opertions, top level, director of regional opertions. Human resource department has the lower level, payroll assistant, the middle level, benefits counselor and benefits manager, the top level, HR director.

In this organization, the administrative assistatns, perform similiar administrative tasks across departments and do not handle function-specific tasks , e.g. HR. Thus, this organization's administrative assiatant ought be suggested grouping the front-line administrative jobs in a separate job family called office support. However, in some organizations, administrative assistant has possible to need to handle function-specific tasks, e.g. HR. Hence, in these organizations administrative assitant can be the low level group to HR department.

In the job evaluation step, this organization chooses to apply point method to evaluate the pay worth to every job title. The evaluation points method can be weights for example the four degrees for education level are identified as below:

1=high school, 2=assocaites, 3= bacholors, 4=master/graduate points are then calculated by multiplying the degree by the weights.

The compensable factor for the evaluation for front desk receiptionist as below:

skill (50%) degree(1,2,3,4) weight points

education level 1 25% 25

degree of

technical skills 1 25% 25

responsibility(30%)

scope of control 1 10% 10

impact of job 2 20% 40

degree of

problem solving 1 10% 10

task complexity 1 10% 10

120

The ensure that the pay structure is extremely competitive, a pay survey will be conducted. The market pay data must be from the relevant labor market. Surveys can include i.e. six organizations who recruit and hire similiar jobs in the regions. Base pay salary data from the responding organizations are reflected to ensure the summary job descriptions , sample data are appropriately similiar to those in this organization in order to compare and analyze the pay data between other similiar organizations and this organization.

Finally , it need to implement how to design the pay structure. it can be setted the pay ranges for each pay grade, pay ranges create upper and lower pay rates for each job in the pay scale. Each pay grade will have a minimum and maximum pay rate. It is important to remember that all jobs in a paygrade will have the same minimum and maximum pay rates. Percent guidelines below the midpoint the pay range will reach . For example, the maximum might be 10% percent above the midpoint and the minimum might be 10% below the midpoint. The percent guidelines can be based on imput from the organization's job evaluation committee, e.g. clerical and office positions: 10% above and below the midpoint. Entery to mid-level professional and management positions: 30 % above and below the midpoint.

reference

Milkovich, G., & Newman, J. (2008). Compensation,
MC Graw-Hill Irwin. 0*NET. Available at http:// online.onetcenter.org

Reward management in a business organisation is basically the way in which that particular business forms and implements strategies and policies to reward the employees to a fair standard and in accordance with how the organisation values them. Reward management in a business organisation usually consists of the business analysing and controlling the employee's remuneration and all of the other benefits for the employees.

The main aim of reward management in a business organisation is to reward the employees fairly for the work that they have completed. The main reason reward management exists in business organisations is to motivate the employees in that particular organisation to work hard and try their best to achieve the goals which are set out by the business. Reward management in business organisations not only consist of financial rewards such as pay but they also consist of non-financial rewards such as employee recognition, employee training/development and increased job responsibility.

Reward management in a business organisation deals with the design, implementation and maintenance of reward practices that are geared towards the improvement of the business organisations performance.

The Importance of Reward Management

The elements of reward management within a business organisation are all the things that they use to attract potential employees into their business which includes salary, bonuses, incentive pay, benefits and employee growth opportunities such as professional development and training opportunities.

Having a reward management system in place provides the business with many advantages, especially in small to medium size organisations where the managers must have a good relationship with the employees. Reward programmes have proved to be very successful in motivating employees and in turn increase the performance of the organisation as a whole.

Below are some of the reasons why a reward system is important:

Mutually beneficial- A reward system is beneficial not only to the employee but also to the organisation. The employee will feel more motivated to work harder.by having a reward system in place the employee will feel more committed to their work and their productivity will increase. An increase in productivity will then benefit the organisation. Therefore a reward system is mutually beneficial to the employee and the organisation.

Motivation-A reward system will motivate employees by reaching targets and organisational goals in exchange for rewards. A reward system is great at motivating employees but they will also be motivated to prove themselves to the organisation.

Absenteeism-A reward system will reduce absenteeism in the organisation. Employees like being rewarded for a job well done and if there is a reward system in place, employees will be less likely to be ringing in sick and not showing up for work. Also by having a reward system in place the employees will be clearer about the targets and goals of the organisation as they will be rewarded when reach certain targets. So by having a reward system as an incentive they will be less likely to be absent from work.

Loyalty-A reward system will increase the employee's loyalty to the organisation. By a reward system being in place the employee feels valued by the organisation and knows that their opinion matters. If an employee is happy with the reward system, they are more likely to appreciate work place and remain loyal to the organisation

Morale-Having a reward system in place providing employees with incentives and recognition will boost their morale. By encouraging employees to meet goals and targets it gives them clear focus and purpose which will their morale. By the employees morale being boosted this will increase the morale of the entire organisation. This is all down to a reward system in the organisation.

Teamwork- The reward system will increase the teamwork spirit in the organisation. The reward system will promote teamwork to the employees. The employees will work together as part of a team to achieve their targets in return for rewards. Teamwork within the organisation will help increase efficiency and create a happier workplace. This is another reason why reward systems are important in business organisations.

Types of Reward Systems

There are several ways to classify rewards; the three most common types are as follows:

Intrinsic Rewards Vs Extrinsic Rewards-

Intrinsic rewards are the personal satisfaction you get from the job itself eg having pride in your work, having a feeling of accomplishment or being part of a team. If an employee experiences feelings of achievement or personal growth from the job, this would be labelled as an intrinsic reward.

Extrinsic rewards would include money, promotions and other benefits. Extrinsic rewards are external to the job and come from an outside source, usually management. If an employee receives a salary increase or a promotion, this would be labelled as an extrinsic reward.

Financial Rewards Vs Non-Financial Rewards-

Financial rewards are those that will enhance the employees financial well-being directly eg bonus, increase in wages and profit sharing schemes.

Non-financial rewards do not enhance the employee's financial position directly but make the job more attractive. Some of the Non-financial rewards that a business organisation offer might include-an attractive pension scheme, access to private medical care, help with long-term sickness, crèche facilities, counselling services, staff restaurant etc.

Performance-Based Rewards Vs Membership-Based Rewards-

The rewards that a business organisation gives to their employees can be based on either their performance or membership criteria. Performance-based rewards are exemplified by the use of commissions, piecework pay plans, incentive schemes, group bonuses, merit pay or other forms of pay for performance plans.

Membership-based rewards would include cost of living increases, benefits and salary increase, seniority or time in rank, credentials or future potential.

Case Study

Tom Warner owned a plumbing, heating and air-conditioning business in Montgomery County,Maryland. In the early 1990s, he faced a major problem. His main customers were commercial property management businesses and they wanted to cut costs. In order to do this; these commercial property management businesses decided to end their contract with Tom Warner and hire their own "handymen".

Tom Warner didn't want to lay off any of his 250-person workforce. He decided to reconstruct his workforce into territories. He assigned each worker their own territory and told them to operate their territory as if they were running their own business. He put each "area director" through training in sales techniques, budgeting, negotiating, cost estimating and how to handle customer complaints.

Warner believed that if he had technically superb, friendly, and ambitious employees, they could successfully operate like small-town "handymen", even though they would be part of a large organisation.

Tom Warner's programme proved to be very successful. The area directors developed a strong sense of pride and ownership in their territories. Each employee was able to schedule their own work, handle their own equipment, develop their own estimates and advertising campaigns. These were the rewards that each employee desired.

Tom Warner's programed increased the employees' wages. A typical employee working for Warner before he introduced the programme was earning $60,000.In the first year of the programme that employee was earning $100,000.In the second year he was earning $125,000.

From a reward point of view, Warner's employees are extremely happy and Tom Warner's business grew by more than 200 per cent in 24 months.

Literary Review

According to the book "Human Resource Management in Ireland" 3rd edition by Patrick Gunnigle, Noreen Heraty and Michael j. Morley:

Schuler (1995) outlines a number of core objectives that a business organisation should have in relation to the reward package that they offer.

Schuler states that in order for a business organisations reward package to be successful it must meet the following objectives:

It should attract potential employees- along with the organisations human resource plan and recruitment and selection techniques the reward package should make potential employees want to work there. The reward package including its mix of pay, incentives and benefits should serve to attract suitable potential employees.

It should assist in retaining good employees- the reward package must be perceived internally by the employees as fair and equitable and it should be perceived externally as competitive. Internally the employees should feel happy with the reward package and they should know that in comparison to other businesses it is a very competitive reward package so they won't want to leave and seek employment elsewhere.

It should motivate employees- the reward package should help and assist motivating employees to work harder. By linking rewards to performance it should motivate employees to work harder as there is an incentive element.

It should contribute to human resource and strategic business plans- the reward package should create a rewarding and supportive climate to work in and therefore it should be perceived as an attractive place to work. This will benefit the business as it will be attracting the best applicants.

Reward management in business organisations is extremely important as the reward package helps to attract employees, retain employees and influence performance and behaviour at work.

According to the book "People Management and Development; Human Resource Management at Work" by Mick Marchington and Adrian Wilkinson:

Lawler (1984) feels that a reward system within the business organisation can influence a number of HR processes and practices, which then have a direct impact on the organisations performance as a whole.

Influence recruitment and retention: Lawler states that any business organisations that have a reward system in place will attract and retain the most people. If better performers are rewarded more highly than poor performers. This also will have an effect on recruitment and retention, so performance-based systems are more likely to attract high-performers.

For Example: If a business organisation rewards their employees with high wages, they will attract more applicants which will allow the business more of a choice over selection and hiring decisions. This hopefully will reduce labour turnover in the organisation.

Influence Motivation: Employees see that by having a reward system in place, it puts an importance on various activities and tasks. Reward systems therefore have a motivational impact on the employees. However the management must integrate the reward system with the behaviour they expect from the employees.

Influence Corporate Culture: The way in which the employees are rewarded will have a huge influence on the corporate culture of the organisation.

For example: If a business organisation has a reward system in place that provides benefits for long-serving staff, this will likely shape the existing culture into one where loyalty is seen as central to the business organisations ideology. In contrast, if a business organisation has a reward system in place that rewards the employees for innovative behaviour and ideas, this is more likely to shape the businesses corporate culture into one where creativity and innovation is important.

Cost as an influence: Cost is a huge factor and influence in the reward system. Some business organisations may not be able to afford to set up and maintain the reward system; it may be too costly for them. On the other hand, some business organisations may not want to waste the money on a reward system. This may demotivate the employees as they will think that not worth it and this will have a direct impact on their performance in the organisation which in turn will in turn have a direct impact on the organisations performance as a whole.

According to the book "Human resource management in Ireland" 4th edition by Patrick Gunnigle, Noreen Heraty and Michael j. Morley:

Lawler (1977) highlights that in order for reward management to be successful the reward system needs to have the essential characteristics:

Reward level- In order for reward management to be successful, the reward package must satisfy the employees basic needs for survival, security and self-development.

Individuality- Along with satisfying the employee's basic needs, the reward system should be flexible enough to meet the employees varying individual needs.

Internal equity- The rewards must be seen as fair when compared to others in the business. The criteria and reasons for the allocation of rewards to employees should be equitable and clear to everyone in the organisation .The reason behind the allocation of rewards to employees should be communicated and accepted by all parties. The rewards should be applied consistently throughout the organisation.

External equity- The rewards must be seen as fair when compared to those offered for comparable work outside the organisation.

Trust- In order for reward management to be successful in the organisation, the management and the employees must believe in the reward system 100 per cent. The employees must believe and accept that will receive rewards when they meet the relevant criteria. The management should trust that the employees will perform at a high standard and the best to their ability in return for rewards.

According to Lawler (1977) in order for a business organisation to be successful in reward management, he believes that a reward system must have the characteristics listed above.

According to the book "Human resource management" 6th edition by De Cenzo and Robbins:

Armstrong and Murlis (1998) offer some broad distinctions between the main types of reward system:

Gain Sharing Schemes-the pay of a group of workers is linked to improvements in internal company productivity.

Employee Stock Ownership Schemes (ESOPs)-The business organisation offers company stock (at a lower rate than normal) to certain employees.

Profit-Sharing Schemes-The business organisation gives a certain percentage of the end of year profits to the employees.

Skill-Based Pay Schemes-The business organisation rewards the employees with pay on the basis of job-related skills or competencies.

Individual Incentive Schemes-The business organisation rewards the employees for reaching or exceeding specific established performance criteria. Piece- rate schemes are the most obvious form of individual performance related rewards.

Group Incentive Schemes-The business organisation rewards groups of employees with the same principles they use on individual schemes. Used most commonly when group work or team work is present in the business organisation.

Conclusion

To conclude I am going to give a brief run through the topics I have covered throughout this report.

I defined and explained the meaning of what reward management is and how organisations manage rewards in organisations. I then went on to discuss the importance of reward management within organisations, by doing this I pointed out the advantages of having reward systems in an organisation. These benefits included mutually beneficial, increases motivation, improves morale, increases the employees loyalty to the organisation, improves teamwork and reduces absenteeism. I looked at commonly used reward schemes. I looked at a case study about Tom Warner was forced to reward his employees with a huge amount of responsibility; however it had an extremely successful outcome for him. I then looked at the main aims that every reward system should have; attract potential employees, assist in retaining good employees, motivate employees, contribute to human resource and strategic business plans. I explained the direct impact a reward system can have on the organisation as a whole ie influence on performance, influence on motivation, influence on the corporate culture.

I looked at and explained the essential characteristics a reward system must have in order to be effective. This is important for management when designing their reward system. They should look at and evaluate their current reward system and make sure it possesses the right characteristics. I then differentiated between the most common types of reward schemes according to research I found on Armstrong and Murlis' point of view on reward systems.

Reward management is concerned with the formulation and implementation of strategies and policies that aim to reward people fairly, equitably and consistently in accordance with their value to the organization.

Reward management consists of analysing and controlling employee remuneration, compensation and all of the other benefits for the employees. Reward management aims to create and efficiently operate a reward structure for an organisation. Reward structure usually consists of pay policy and practices, salary and payroll administration, total reward, minimum wage, executive pay and team reward.

Reward management is a popular management topic. Reward management was developed on the basis of psychologists' behavioral research. Psychologists started studying behavior in the early 1900s; one of the first psychologists to study behavior was Sigmund Freud and his work was called the Psychoanalytic Theory. Many other behavioral psychologists improved and added onto his work. With the improvements in the behavioral research and theories, psychologists started looking at how people reacted to rewards and what motivated them to do what they were doing, and as a result of this, psychologists started creating motivational theories, which is very closely affiliated with reward management.

Defining motivation as "the degree to which an individual wants and choose to engage in certain specific behaviours", to which Vroom (quoted in Mitchell, 1982) adds that performance = ability x motivation. To have an efficient Reward System then, is mandatory that employees know exactly what their task is, have the skills to do it, have the necessary motivation and work in an environment allowing the transformation of intended actions into an actual behaviour. From the company point of view instead, an effective performance appraisal has to be present, in order to let motivation be a major contributor to the rewarded performance

Objective[edit]

Reward management deals with processes, policies and strategies which are required to guarantee that the contribution of employees to the business is recognized by all means. Objective of reward management is to reward employees fairly, equitably and consistently in correlation to the value of these individuals to the organization. Reward system exists in order to motivate employees to work towards achieving strategic goals which are set by entities. Reward management is not only concerned with pay and employee benefits. It is equally concerned with non-financial rewards such as recognition, training, development and increased job responsibility.

Kerr (1995) brings to attention how Reward Management is an easily understandable concept in theory, but how its practical application results often difficult. The author, in fact, points up how frequently the company creates a Reward System hoping to reward a specific behavior, but ending up rewarding another one. The example made is the one of a company giving an annual merit increase to all its employees, differentiating just between an "outstanding" (+5%), "above average" (+4%) and "negligent" (+3%) workers. Because the difference between the percentage increasing was so slight, what the company obtained from the employees was indifference to the extra percentage point for a superlative job or the loss of one point for an irresponsible behavior. In the following table other common management errors are summarized.

Rewards serve many purposes in organisations. They serve to build a better employment deal, hold on to good employees and to reduce employee turnover.

The principal goal is to increase people's willingness to work in one's company, to enhance their productivity.

Most people assimilate "rewards", with salary raise or bonuses, but this is only one kind of reward, extrinsic reward. Studies proves that salespeople prefer pay raises because they feel frustrated by their inability to obtain other rewards,[8] but this behavior can be modified by applying a complete reward strategy.

There are two kinds of rewards:

Extrinsic rewards: concrete rewards that employee receive. Bonuses: Usually annually, Bonuses motivates the employee to put in all endeavours and efforts during the year to achieve more than a satisfactory appraisal that increases the chance of earning several salaries as lump sum. The scheme of bonuses varies within organizations; some organizations ensure fixed bonuses which eliminate the element of asymmetric information, conversely, other organizations deal with bonuses in terms of performance which is subjective and may develop some sort of bias which may discourage employees and create setback. Therefore, managers must be extra cautious and unbiased.

Salary raise: Is achieved after hard work and effort of employees, attaining and acquiring new skills or academic certificates and as appreciation for employees duty (yearly increments) in an organization. This type of reward is beneficial for the reason that it motivates employees in developing their skills and competence which is also an investment for the organization due to increased productivity and performance. This type of reward offers long-term satisfaction to employees. Nevertheless, managers must also be fair and equal with employees serving the organization and eliminate the possibility of adverse selection where some employees can be treated superior or inferior to others.

Gifts: Are considered short-term. Mainly presented as a token of appreciation for an achievement or obtaining an organizations desired goal. Any employee would appreciate a tangible matter that boosts their self-esteem for the reason of recognition and appreciation from the management. This type of reward basically provides a clear vision of the employee's correct path and motivates employee into stabilising or increasing their efforts to achieve higher returns and attainments. Monetary gifts, such as Gift cards are also more likely to be used for luxury purchases and can build an emotional bond with the organisation.[9]

Promotion: Quite similar to the former type of reward. Promotions tend to effect the long-term satisfaction of employees. This can be done by elevating the employee to a higher stage and offering a title with increased accountability and responsibility due to employee efforts, behaviour and period serving a specific organization. This type of reward is vital for the main reason of redundancy and routine. The employee is motivated in this type of reward to contribute all his efforts in order to gain managements trust and acquire their delegation and responsibility. The issue revolved around promotion is adverse selection and managers must be fair and reasonable in promoting their employees.

Other kinds of tangible rewards

Intrinsic rewards: tend to give personal satisfaction to individual[10]

Information / feedback: Also a significant type of reward that successful and effective managers never neglect. This type of rewards offers guidance to employees whether positive (remain on track) or negative (guidance to the correct path). This also creates a bond and adds value to the relationship of managers and employees.

Recognition: Is recognizing an employee's performance by verbal appreciation. This type of reward may take the presence of being formal for example meeting or informal such as a "pat on the back" to boost employees self-esteem and happiness which will result in additional contributing efforts.

Trust/empowerment: in any society or organization, trust is a vital aspect between living individuals in order to add value to any relationship. This form of reliance is essential in order to complete tasks successfully. Also, takes place in empowerment when managers delegate tasks to employees. This adds importance to an employee where his decisions and actions are reflected. Therefore, this reward may benefit organizations for the idea of two minds better than one.

Intrinsic rewards makes the employee feel better in the organization, while Extrinsic rewards focus on the performance and activities of the employee in order to attain a certain outcome. The principal difficulty is to find a balance between employees' performance (extrinsic) and happiness (intrinsic).

The reward also needs to be according to the employee's personality. For instance, a sports fan will be really happy to get some tickets for the next big match. However a mother who passes all her time with her children, may not use them and therefore they will be wasted.

When rewarding one, the manager needs to choose if he wants to rewards an Individual, a Team or a whole Organization. One will choose the reward scope in harmony with the work that has been achieved.

Individual Base pay, incentives, benefits

Rewards attendance, performance, competence

Team: team bonus, rewards group cooperation

Organization: profit-sharing, shares, gain-sharing

An interpretation of Maslow's hierarchy of needs, represented as a pyramid with the more basic needs at the bottom[12]

Motivational theories are split into two groups as process and content theories. Content theories endeavor to name and analyze the factors which motivate people to perform better and more efficiently while process theories concentrate on how different types of personal traits interfere and impact the human behavior.[13] Content theories are highly related with extrinsic rewards, things that are concrete like bonuses and will help improve employees' physiological circumstances whereas process theories are concerned with intrinsic rewards, such as recognition and respect, which will help boost employees confidence in the work place and improve job satisfaction.[14]

A famous content theory would be Maslow's Hierarchy of Needs,[15] and a famous process theory would be the equity theory.[16]

Theories of motivation provide a theoretical basis for reward management though some of the best known ones have emerged from the psychology discipline. Perhaps the first and best known of these comes from the work of Abraham Maslow.[17] Maslow's Hierarchy of Needs describes a pyramid comprising a series of layers from at the base the most fundamental physiological needs such as food, water, shelter and sex, rising to the apex where self-actualisation needs included morality and creativity.

Maslow saw these levels of needs being fulfilled one at a time in sequence from bottom to top. Employment and the resources it brings are classed under 'safety needs' (level 2) while the workplace may also contribute to a sense of 'belonging' (level 3) and recognition at work can satisfy the need for 'self-esteem' (level 4).

Frederick Herzberg's motivator-hygiene theory, first published in 1959, argues that an employee's job satisfaction or dissatisfaction is influenced by two distinct sets of factors and also that satisfaction and dissatisfaction were not at opposite ends of the same continuum but instead needed to be measured separately. The two sets of factors are motivator factors and hygiene factors. According to Herzberg, real motivation comes from the work itself, from completing tasks, while the role of reward is to prevent dissatisfaction arising.[18]

Expectancy theory is the theory which posits that we select our behaviour based on the desirability of expected outcomes of the action. It was most prominently used in a work context by Victor Vroom [19] who sought to establish the relationship between performance, motivation and ability and expressed it as a multiplicative one – where performance equals motivation x ability. There are a lot of attractions for this kind of approach, particularly for employers who can target their motivation effort and anticipate a definable mathematical return for them. As this is a cognitive process theory it relies on the way employees perceive rewards These three theories plus variants of them have been used in countless research studies and continue to inform the practice of reward management up to the present day.

Job evaluation[edit]

Job evaluation is closely related to reward management. It is important to understand and identify a job's order of importance. Job evaluation is the process in which jobs are systematically assessed to one another within an organization in order to define the worth and value of the job, to ensure the principle of equal pay for equal work. In the United Kingdom, it is now illegal to discriminate workers' pay levels and benefits, employment terms and conditions and promotion opportunities.[20] Job evaluation is one method that can be adopted by companies in order to make sure that discrimination is eliminated and that the work performed is rewarded with fair pay scales. This system carries crucial importance for managers to decide which rewards should be handed out by what amount and to whom. Job evaluation provides the basis for grading, pay structure, grading jobs in the structure and managing job and pay relativities.[21]

It has been said that fairness and objectivity are the core principles using an assessment of the nature and size of the job each is employed to carry out.[22]

There are many different methods of job evaluation which can be used, but the three simplest methods are ranking, classification and factor comparison.[23] However, there are more complex variations of methods such as the point method which uses scales to measure job factors. This method does not rank employees against one another but looks at the job as a whole. A disadvantage of these methods of job evaluation are that they are very static and it would be very difficult to perform a job evaluation quickly if it was needed.[citation needed]

Acas has stated that there were five main reasons why employers look at performing a job evaluation. These include: When deciding on a pay scale: Making sure that the current system is fair and equal for employees, Deciding on benefits such as bonuses, Comparing pay against other companies and reviewing all jobs after a major company pay change.[24] Employees need to feel that they are being paid a fair wage compared to the same job with the competition. If this is true it may help reduce staff turnover which is very beneficial for employers as it reduces the cost of hiring new staff.

Research regarding job evaluation has mainly been conducted using qualitative data collection methods such as interviews, large scale surveys and basic experimental methods. Therefore, there is a large gap for research on job evaluation collecting quantitative data for a more statistical analysis. A comparison between public and private sectors and the methods of job evaluation is another area that should be considered for further research.

However, is job evaluation enough? Steinburg (1999) [25] stated that very few organisations take into account that job evaluation should also look at emotional labour that may be used by employees.

Performance appraisal is the method in which an employee's job performance is evaluated and reviewed.[26] This compares employee work behaviour with the organisations pre-set standards to provide feedback on job performance. Performance appraisals are a form of motivation through either positive or negative reinforcement, depending on outcome. Typically this information is gained through interview and questionnaire functions annually, executed among management of larger organisations primarily, as a method of motivation to gain full potential of staff.[27] The goal of which is to align and manage all organisational resources "to achieve highest possible performance" by improving your current staff through encouragement, setting targets and improving on past mistakes.[28] Edward Lawler of the University of Southern California unveiled research showing that 93% percent of companies use annual appraisal [29]

Performance appraisal was set up in the first place, as a justification for the pay of an employee. If his performance was seen as insufficient, his pay would be cut down. However, if it was seen of a higher quality, he could receive a pay rise. Performance appraisals have been described as a "flawed system", One must ask, can an entire year's work be reviewed at one point in time? It has been argued that the time, money and energy needed is not comparable to its effectiveness.[30] There are various appraisal methods.

Some of these include « rank and yank » by which an organisation ranks its employees against each other and terminates the employment of the employee who finishes at bottom place. That corresponds to the yanking. Then there is the critical incident technique by which the organisation collects information and observes human behaviour that have a strong impact either positive or negative on an activity or procedure.

Each employee is different and can bring in something special to the organisation. Each employee has a specific job to fulfil. Performance appraisals are needed in order to understand how every employee can produce the best performance.

Improve performance: performance improvement is the notion of measuring the productivity of a certain procedure, and then finding solutions in order for the productivity to rise, the capability of the employees and their effectiveness.[31]

Increase motivation: Performance appraisal is used as a motivation tool. An employee's efficiency can be proven if the targets he was set, have been achieved. The employee will be motivated to do even better and his performance will rise in the near future.[32]

Identify training/development needs: The fundamental step of training and development is establishing the organisational needs for the employees at this time and in the near future. A few questions may be asked in the process: What can an employee learn in order to be more productive? In which field is training most necessary? And finally who should benefit from the training most?

The effectiveness of an employee is the key factor for the employer, because the profit the company or organisation makes depends on the employees' productiveness.

The training and development needs should begin with an assessment of the company as it lies currently, how it operates and what each employee is best at. This assessment will enable the training to be based on certain factors which seem most important. Knowledge of the organisation's strategic plan and its needs for the future must help the training to bring the company up a step on the ladder.[33] In using a performance appraisal, an organisation can build an employee profile of poor performances which allows a reduced risk of legal implications for redundancies. Seeing additional benefit, as the company can decide who is worthy of promotion or bonus'.[30]

Manage careers: career management . Managing your career efficiently involves a list of various factors which need to be referred to as often as possible: taking into account the goals you have giving yourself all along your professional career, allowing yourself to have a comfortable lifestyle and by feeling some level of personal accomplishment when you look back at what you have done. These three factors are key to a productive career.

INSIGHT

There is absolutely no one in the world who doesn't like being rewarded and recognized for the hard work they do and the same holds true for employees of your workplace as well. Employee recognition is the acknowledgment of an employee's efforts, hard work and behavior at the workplace that have contributed to the organization's success and objectives in some way. Both things are very important: recognizing and acknowledging these efforts, as well as rewarding employees for their fruitful efforts. Here are some ways in which you as an employer or business owner can recognize the efforts of your workplace and reward them accordingly:

Day-to-day recognition – It is important to motivate and encourage employees to perform well on an everyday basis and not just on a periodic level. For example, small words of praise, little words of encouragement and constant motivation are highly important to make your employees feel encouraged for their efforts and to maintain a positive flow of the workplace environment.

Informal recognition – Informal recognition is the kind of recognition which includes gestures of encouragement and appreciation. A pat on the back or a word of praise in front of the team can go a long way in boosting the morale of the employees.

Formal recognition – Formal recognition is usually in the form of rewards for service, contribution, and achievements. These recognition forms also include events held for the celebration of achievements. Formal recognition often has some legal and policy requirements.

Importance of Employee recognition

As an employer or business owner, it becomes your responsibility to make sure there is a proper employee recognition program in your organization. Such program offers many benefits and, hence, is of high importance. To know what the various benefits of such a program are, you can go through the following given information:

Encourage engagement – One of the ways in which recognition of your employee's efforts or hard work can benefit is by encouraging or inspiring further engagement and boosting overall performance. When one gets some praise or pat on the back, he/she automatically tries to give the same level of performance and improves efforts further.

Encourage better business results – The simple gesture of praising or rewarding your employees at work can have a direct impact on your bottom-line and can lead to better overall results that are a consequence of better individual performances.

Increase loyalty & Retain the best talent – When one is recognized for his/her hard work, he/she tends to be more loyal towards you and the work he/she is doing. This is something that can help to retain important and skilled employees in the long run.

Build a supportive work environment – The more your employees feel encouraged and valued, the more will they be supportive to your cause, hence building a supportive and active work environment.

Encourage a sense of ownership of the place in employees – When an employee hears a word of recognition or receives an award for his/her services, he/she begins to feel a sense of belonging and ownership for the workplace, which further improves performance and infuses a sense of positivity in the environment.

INFORMAL WAYS TO REWARD YOUR EMPLOYEES

Besides the formal ways to award and reward employees and recognize their hard work, there are endless informal ways or gestures that can say and express that you are proud of the way an employee has performed and encourage the efforts. But since these methods are merely gestures, you and your managers must make sure that they in no way are out of the bounds of the workplace culture and policies. They must be polite, subtle, suitable to the interest of the various employees and not bothersome or out of line in any way the following are some of the informal ways to recognize the well-performed job/tasks of your employees:

A well-meant and simple thank you to your employee on a job or task that has been performed well is enough to say that you are appreciative of the efforts. Say thank you often and mean it each time you say it.

Sending a personal note or an email can also prove to be a great gesture and may infuse a lot of confidence and gratitude in the employees.

If your employee receives positive comments from clients or seniors, do make sure that you let him know about it to boost his morale and motivate him to perform well in the future also.

Create a monthly or weekly employee honor roll in the office and paste pictures or names of employees who have worked particularly well during that time period.

Praise the employee who has performed well in front of the team to encourage not just him but also others to perform well.

Take your team out for lunch or dinner after they have accomplished a particular deal or finished a project successfully.

Allow employees who work hard and perform well to attend special meetings or give them special tasks as a gesture for their excellent contribution.

Set up a point system for loyalty, punctuality, team work, attendance and other such factors and start rating employees on a per month basis. The employee who scores the maximum can be sent a small treat, coupon or a goodie bag to encourage everyone at the workplace to aim for the highest score.

Give examples of the achievements of the few hardworking employees to others in front of them to indirectly praise them and boost their morale and reputation in the office.

Allow the employee to take long lunch breaks once in a while or sanction a leave as a recognition of good work on other occasions.

Create titles like 'most hardworking employee of the month', 'most punctual employee of the month' and 'the most reliable employee of the month' etc. and distribute these titles with a small pack of chocolate etc. at the end of each month to boost performance and encourage individual skills and qualities.

Always thank or appreciate employees for their ideas and suggestions that can help the organization even in the smallest of ways. This boosts a feeling of giving opinions among employees and reduces the hesitation that one might feel at the workplace as far as speaking up in front of other workers is concerned.

Always appreciate those who stay back long hours to complete their work, irrespective of whether that was required or not. This avoids unnecessary frustrations and resentment for you or the workplace in general among employees.

Always greet employees at the starting of the day or whenever you encounter them in the workplace. An employer who is cold or doesn't respond well to the employees' greetings may be seen as unappreciative, and this can have a negative impact on workers.

Reference

Leon, M. (2002). High performers, how the best companies find and keep them, Jossey -Bass, John Wiley & Sons, Inc, US pp.133-134

In compensation and benefits reward management aspect, it is not possible to imagine an offer of employment that does not indicate a salary or wage and possibly other terms of compensation as well as description of the various benefits available with the employment. So, a candidate accepts ot rejects the job offer, he/she will regard how a compensation package with a monetary of non-monetary value, such as a fair exchange for whose labor. So, the award management plan will include monetary reward and non-monetary reward both is better than monetary reward only. For example, piece rate py is good for factory workers, commissions have long been a major part of the compensation of salepeople and merit pay and bonuses are well established methods of rewarding good performance for car salepeople. So, the variable or incentive pay is a good reward implementation plan for salespeople, insurance agents.

How to evaluate the base pay level is the more accurate? Leon, M. (2002) indicated that when a company needs to determine levels of base pay, the best companies have several objectives. The most important , in a global business environment characteristized by strong demand for talented experienced employees is to be competitive. The determination of base pay level does not depend on only in one's own industry, but also in other industries competing for the same talent. In fact, a firm's closes competition for human resources often is not its closet industrial competitor. In addition, the best companies are attractive to the levels of compensation appropriate to the different regions and countries where facilites are located or where workers originate. At the same time, some are developing truly global talent managers, whose pay scales are most pay level to similar manager in other companies than they are with typical rate of pay in either the firm's headquarter country or its overseas locations.

Reward management systems have major impact on organization capability to catch, retain and motivate high potential employees and as a result getting the high level of performance. I also believe reward of employee performance can lead to differentiation between the productivity of the bank employees. In fact, bank employee performance is originally what on employee does or does not do. Performance of employees could include quantity of output, quality of output, timliness of output, presence at work, cooperativeness.

Reward management in bank serrvice industry, bank orgnization needs have effective and attractive reward management system to attract talent human resource applications. But banks are facing global saving bank competition. Reward management system is a core function of human resource discipline and is a strategic partner with company management. An good reward management can raise bank service employees performance in loan, saving mortgage etc. different departments.

An effective reward management system can shorten service timeliness to raise talent employee individual bank service performance, raise the talent employee team cooperative effort in loan, mortgage, counter etc. different service departments.

However, reward management system tool includes both financial and non-financial reards which are also called as extrinsic and intrinsic rewards. In bank industry financial rewards include salary increase, bonus, commission, housing loan allowance, education loan allowance. The non-financial rewards include promotion and title, authority and responsibility, appreciation and praise, participation to decisions, vacation time, comfort of working place, social authority, customer and management positive oral and written feedback, flexible working hours, design of work recognition , social rights, etc.

Property management industry reward management practitioners include property managers, caretakers, attendants, security guards, facility maintenance workers and cleaners. It is essential for employers to formulate strategic plans and coordinate labor relations of human resource with the development. In respons to the people-related challenge and opportunities to property management industry. It includes six aspects: communicating and improving staff benefits, promoting work-life balance and health and enhancing work arrangements, enhancing staff's career development and promotion prospect, improving the professional image of the industry, friendly employment practices for mature persons. Through these practices enterprises can make their job vacancie about attractive and answer misunderstandings about the property management industry.

Thus, the manpower shortage challenge will be avoid , when the people have interest to join the industry and they feel the reward is attractive to them to develop career. How to improve staff benefit? It includes new recruit entry bonus schemes, giving out little gifts and bonuses, during celebrations and festive occasions, and granting gratuities to critically ill employees or on the death of the employee's immediate family members, offers employees insurance plans, offering award schemes for employee's children by granting scholarships to outstanding students in recognition of their excellent exchange scholarships are available to subsidise their children's study abroad, promoting working-life balance to staff, such as organizing interest classes, setting up sports teams, organizing gatherings, participating in charitable activities, encouraging employees to organize social gatherings, promoting happiness at work, strengthening occupational safety and health arrangements to employees, e.g. setting up occupational safety and health committee / departments, formulating occupational safety and health policies, entertainment of work arrangement: compressed working days, five-day work week, flexible working days, flexible rostering, job sharing, part time work pattern, most rest time for frontline employee, job nature or workflow modification / re-engineering, improvement of employee's workplace environment, intra-district redeployment.

Reward is an important element in information technology industry. The IT industry had been needing a leader in changing traditional compensation strategy. Pay for performance needs to be designed effective reward system to encourage IT employee to work hardly in order to reward and contribute the most to an IT organization's technological productivity and profits.

The compensation mix depends on deliverable and the impact it has on the IT business. Consequently higher the responsibility greater the variable content in the pay package. IT industry has many IT professionals , such as programmers, software or hardware engineers, e-commerce website designer etc. different IT professionals. Hence, different IT professionals need have different skills to evaluate pay performace level fairly. However, performance related pay plans, it is a motivator the improves productivity. It helps in improving IT product productivity and performance levels when making every IT professional individual equally to encourage or motivate themm work to hardly in their IT unique professional aspects. It is a greater motivator for top performances and teams as they can get fair and reasonable reward and pay according to their contributions.

In fact, there is no standard formula for a performance -related incentive plan, it is unique for each IT professional. However, the incentive plan should need to be design to each IT professional with an organization's objectives. They include, communication and understanding of objectives, consideration of different IT professional performnce against objectives, translating evaluation into the kid of IT professional performance rating, a link between ratings and pay to the kind of IT unique professional skill.

What is reward management strategic principle to employment relationship? employees needs to pay tangibles (salary, wage, cars, educational , holiday allowance etc.) or/and intangible (recognition, career development growth etc.) rewards to employees aim. Individual balance to achieve tangible output, sales and/or intangibles loyalty , service performance, commitment. Hence, reward managment forms the employment relationship, if an HR manager is to succeed in successully managing the employment relationship, he/she will have to do well in reward managment.

The reward management principle includes simplicity, it must be easily understood by everyone in the organization, fairness and equitability , every component of the system must be justifiable applied. This element is arguably the most challenging to implement and is the cause of most reward management related problems , such as strike, turnover, dissatisfaction etc. Hence, an attractive communication and training to the low skilful labour to have chance to upgrade high skilful which is needed, a participatory chance is effective one should ideally be negatiated and agreed between management and employees.

In fact, traditionally companies have always adopted the base pay strategy. It pays the legal minimum wages and salaries. However, it does not adequate in new work cultures and in terms of attracting , retaining and motivating top performers for strategic purposes, but still very commonly uded for lower level employees. The new reward strategic options include as below:

1. Knowledge and skills based strategy, because of the proven relatin job performance, organizations have sought to encourage continuous skills development by trying it to rewards. A organization simply varies its pay structure according to one's level of knowledge and skill (job evaluation systems. It can define which skills, it values and will pay for and must have a supportive training and development strategy. It is based pay with an equal base pay and a variation based on skills and knowledge. It may be costly in the short-term , but it is beneficial from a knowledge HR base through increased productivity and quality of product.

2. Performance based (varied pay based structure strategy), employees should be rewarded only for the value they create. A company will reward employee in the same grade variably depending on each employee's performance.

3. Incentive based pay structure strategy, it measures but being different in that it focuses on group performance rather than individual performance. The starting point in strategy is to define group performance targets , such as productivity sale volumes or profitability.

What factors can influence organization's reward stragety? They include: Afforability, the argument is that an organization can't borrow to reward employees, but it should reward from the value created by the employees themselves; legislation sets the minimum base pay minumum fixed pay rate; union/workers committees' pay level are determined through collecting bargaining. For example, strike issue will bring higher salary level in possible; external job value, the market value of the job, e.g. what is the market value of an HR manager or clerical assistant; internal job value, perceived value of job compared to the other jobs which the organization will determine the reward for the jobs , e.g. HR manage compared to finance manager; value of the person, employees holding similar jobs can be paid differently depending on the value to the organization performance; the economy changing factor (labor supply/demand) in labor market, e.g. it is a depressed economy increases the supply of labour, it will reduce the labour wage/salary market prices, due to the economy is bad , employers won't need to raise to any employees number and it has excess labour supply number to affect reward policy strategy.

Reward management in a business organisation is basically the way in which that particular business forms and implements strategies and policies to reward the employees to a fair standard and in accordance with how the organisation values them. Reward management in a business organisation usually consists of the business analysing and controlling the employee's remuneration and all of the other benefits for the employees.

The main aim of reward management in a business organisation is to reward the employees fairly for the work that they have completed. The main reason reward management exists in business organisations is to motivate the employees in that particular organisation to work hard and try their best to achieve the goals which are set out by the business. Reward management in business organisations not only consist of financial rewards such as pay but they also consist of non-financial rewards such as employee recognition, employee training/development and increased job responsibility.

Reward management in a business organisation deals with the design, implementation and maintenance of reward practices that are geared towards the improvement of the business organisations performance.

The Importance of Reward Management

The elements of reward management within a business organisation are all the things that they use to attract potential employees into their business which includes salary, bonuses, incentive pay, benefits and employee growth opportunities such as professional development and training opportunities. Having a reward management system in place provides the business with many advantages, especially in small to medium size organisations where the managers must have a good relationship with the employees. Reward programmes have proved to be very successful in motivating employees and in turn increase the performance of the organisation as a whole.

Below are some of the reasons why a reward system is important:

Mutually beneficial- A reward system is beneficial not only to the employee but also to the organisation. The employee will feel more motivated to work harder.by having a reward system in place the employee will feel more committed to their work and their productivity will increase. An increase in productivity will then benefit the organisation. Therefore a reward system is mutually beneficial to the employee and the organisation.

Motivation-A reward system will motivate employees by reaching targets and organisational goals in exchange for rewards. A reward system is great at motivating employees but they will also be motivated to prove themselves to the organisation.

Absenteeism-A reward system will reduce absenteeism in the organisation.

Employees like being rewarded for a job well done and if there is a reward system in place, employees will be less likely to be ringing in sick and not showing up for work. Also by having a reward system in place the employees will be clearer about the targets and goals of the organisation as they will be rewarded when reach certain targets. So by having a reward system as an incentive they will be less likely to be absent from work.

Loyalty-A reward system will increase the employee's loyalty to the organisation. By a reward system being in place the employee feels valued by the organisation and knows that their opinion matters. If an employee is happy with the reward system, they are more likely to appreciate work place and remain loyal to the organisation

Morale-Having a reward system in place providing employees with incentives and recognition will boost their morale. By encouraging employees to meet goals and targets it gives them clear focus and purpose which will their morale. By the employees morale being boosted this will increase the morale of the entire organisation. This is all down to a reward system in the organisation.

Teamwork- The reward system will increase the teamwork spirit in the organisation. The reward system will promote teamwork to the employees. The employees will work together as part of a team to achieve their targets in return for rewards. Teamwork within the organisation will help increase efficiency and create a happier workplace. This is another reason why reward systems are important in business organisations.

Types of Reward Systems

There are several ways to classify rewards; the three most common types are as follows:

Intrinsic Rewards Vs Extrinsic Rewards-

Intrinsic rewards are the personal satisfaction you get from the job itself eg having pride in your work, having a feeling of accomplishment or being part of a team. If an employee experiences feelings of achievement or personal growth from the job, this would be labelled as an intrinsic reward.

Extrinsic rewards would include money, promotions and other benefits. Extrinsic rewards are external to the job and come from an outside source, usually management. If an employee receives a salary increase or a promotion, this would be labelled as an extrinsic reward.

Financial Rewards Vs Non-Financial Rewards-

Financial rewards are those that will enhance the employees financial well-being directly eg bonus, increase in wages and profit sharing schemes.

Non-financial rewards do not enhance the employee's financial position directly but make the job more attractive. Some of the Non-financial rewards that a business organisation offer might include-an attractive pension scheme, access to private medical care, help with long-term sickness, crèche facilities, counselling services, staff restaurant etc.

Performance-Based Rewards Vs Membership-Based Rewards-

The rewards that a business organisation gives to their employees can be based on either their performance or membership criteria. Performance-based rewards are exemplified by the use of commissions, piecework pay plans, incentive schemes, group bonuses, merit pay or other forms of pay for performance plans.

Membership-based rewards would include cost of living increases, benefits and salary increase, seniority or time in rank, credentials or future potential.

Case Study

Tom Warner owned a plumbing, heating and air-conditioning business in Montgomery County,Maryland. In the early 1990s, he faced a major problem. His main customers were commercial property management businesses and they wanted to cut costs. In order to do this; these commercial property management businesses decided to end their contract with Tom Warner and hire their own "handymen".

Tom Warner didn't want to lay off any of his 250-person workforce. He decided to reconstruct his workforce into territories. He assigned each worker their own territory and told them to operate their territory as if they were running their own business. He put each "area director" through training in sales techniques, budgeting, negotiating, cost estimating and how to handle customer complaints.

Warner believed that if he had technically superb, friendly, and ambitious employees, they could successfully operate like small-town "handymen", even though they would be part of a large organisation.

Tom Warner's programme proved to be very successful. The area directors developed a strong sense of pride and ownership in their territories. Each employee was able to schedule their own work, handle their own equipment, develop their own estimates and advertising campaigns. These were the rewards that each employee desired.

Tom Warner's programed increased the employees' wages. A typical employee working for Warner before he introduced the programme was earning $60,000.In the first year of the programme that employee was earning $100,000.In the second year he was earning $125,000.

From a reward point of view, Warner's employees are extremely happy and Tom Warner's business grew by more than 200 per cent in 24 months.

Literary Review

According to the book "Human Resource Management in Ireland" 3rd edition by Patrick Gunnigle, Noreen Heraty and Michael j. Morley:

Schuler (1995) outlines a number of core objectives that a business organisation should have in relation to the reward package that they offer. Schuler states that in order for a business organisations reward package to be successful it must meet the following objectives:

It should attract potential employees- along with the organisations human resource plan and recruitment and selection techniques the reward package should make potential employees want to work there. The reward package including its mix of pay, incentives and benefits should serve to attract suitable potential employees.

It should assist in retaining good employees- the reward package must be perceived internally by the employees as fair and equitable and it should be perceived externally as competitive. Internally the employees should feel happy with the reward package and they should know that in comparison to other businesses it is a very competitive reward package so they won't want to leave and seek employment elsewhere.

It should motivate employees- the reward package should help and assist motivating employees to work harder. By linking rewards to performance it should motivate employees to work harder as there is an incentive element.

It should contribute to human resource and strategic business plans- the reward package should create a rewarding and supportive climate to work in and therefore it should be perceived as an attractive place to work. This will benefit the business as it will be attracting the best applicants.

Reward management in business organisations is extremely important as the reward package helps to attract employees, retain employees and influence performance and behaviour at work.

According to the book "People Management and Development; Human Resource Management at Work" by Mick Marchington and Adrian Wilkinson:

Lawler (1984) feels that a reward system within the business organisation can influence a number of HR processes and practices, which then have a direct impact on the organisations performance as a whole.

Influence recruitment and retention: Lawler states that any business organisations that have a reward system in place will attract and retain the most people. If better performers are rewarded more highly than poor performers. This also will have an effect on recruitment and retention, so performance-based systems are more likely to attract high-performers.

For Example: If a business organisation rewards their employees with high wages, they will attract more applicants which will allow the business more of a choice over selection and hiring decisions. This hopefully will reduce labour turnover in the organisation.

Influence Motivation: Employees see that by having a reward system in place, it puts an importance on various activities and tasks. Reward systems therefore have a motivational impact on the employees. However the management must integrate the reward system with the behaviour they expect from the employees.

Influence Corporate Culture: The way in which the employees are rewarded will have a huge influence on the corporate culture of the organisation.

For example: If a business organisation has a reward system in place that provides benefits for long-serving staff, this will likely shape the existing culture into one where loyalty is seen as central to the business organisations ideology. In contrast, if a business organisation has a reward system in place that rewards the employees for innovative behaviour and ideas, this is more likely to shape the businesses corporate culture into one where creativity and innovation is important.

Cost as an influence: Cost is a huge factor and influence in the reward system. Some business organisations may not be able to afford to set up and maintain the reward system; it may be too costly for them. On the other hand, some business organisations may not want to waste the money on a reward system. This may demotivate the employees as they will think that not worth it and this will have a direct impact on their performance in the organisation which in turn will in turn have a direct impact on the organisations performance as a whole.

According to the book "Human resource management in Ireland" 4th edition by Patrick Gunnigle, Noreen Heraty and Michael j. Morley:

Lawler (1977) highlights that in order for reward management to be successful the reward system needs to have the essential characteristics:

Reward level- In order for reward management to be successful, the reward package must satisfy the employees basic needs for survival, security and self-development.

Individuality- Along with satisfying the employee's basic needs, the reward system should be flexible enough to meet the employees varying individual needs.

Internal equity- The rewards must be seen as fair when compared to others in the business. The criteria and reasons for the allocation of rewards to employees should be equitable and clear to everyone in the organisation .The reason behind the allocation of rewards to employees should be communicated and accepted by all parties. The rewards should be applied consistently throughout the organisation.

External equity- The rewards must be seen as fair when compared to those offered for comparable work outside the organisation.

Trust- In order for reward management to be successful in the organisation, the management and the employees must believe in the reward system 100 per cent. The employees must believe and accept that will receive rewards when they meet the relevant criteria. The management should trust that the employees will perform at a high standard and the best to their ability in return for rewards.

According to Lawler (1977) in order for a business organisation to be successful in reward management, he believes that a reward system must have the characteristics listed above.

According to the book "Human resource management" 6th edition by De Cenzo and Robbins:

Armstrong and Murlis (1998) offer some broad distinctions between the main types of reward system:

Gain Sharing Schemes-the pay of a group of workers is linked to improvements in internal company productivity.

Employee Stock Ownership Schemes (ESOPs)-The business organisation offers company stock (at a lower rate than normal) to certain employees.

Profit-Sharing Schemes-The business organisation gives a certain percentage of the end of year profits to the employees.

Skill-Based Pay Schemes-The business organisation rewards the employees with pay on the basis of job-related skills or competencies.

Individual Incentive Schemes-The business organisation rewards the employees for reaching or exceeding specific established performance criteria. Piece- rate schemes are the most obvious form of individual performance related rewards.

Group Incentive Schemes-The business organisation rewards groups of employees with the same principles they use on individual schemes. Used most commonly when group work or team work is present in the business organisation.

Conclusion

To conclude I am going to give a brief run through the topics I have covered throughout this report.

I defined and explained the meaning of what reward management is and how organisations manage rewards in organisations. I then went on to discuss the importance of reward management within organisations, by doing this I pointed out the advantages of having reward systems in an organisation. These benefits included mutually beneficial, increases motivation, improves morale, increases the employees loyalty to the organisation, improves teamwork and reduces absenteeism. I looked at commonly used reward schemes. I looked at a case study about Tom Warner was forced to reward his employees with a huge amount of responsibility; however it had an extremely successful outcome for him. I then looked at the main aims that every reward system should have; attract potential employees, assist in retaining good employees, motivate employees, contribute to human resource and strategic business plans. I explained the direct impact a reward system can have on the organisation as a whole ie influence on performance, influence on motivation, influence on the corporate culture.

I looked at and explained the essential characteristics a reward system must have in order to be effective. This is important for management when designing their reward system. They should look at and evaluate their current reward system and make sure it possesses the right characteristics. I then differentiated between the most common types of reward schemes according to research I found on Armstrong and Murlis' point of view on reward systems.

Human professionals might create the pay structure for their organization, or they might work with an external compensation consultant. There are several steps to design a pay structure: job analysis, job evaluation, pay survey analysis, pay policy and development and pay structure information (Milkovish, G., & Newman, J. 2008).

Milkovich, G. & Newman, J. (2008) explaines that the pay structure steps include as below:

Step one : Job analysis is the process of studying jobs in an organization. The outcome of this process is a job description that includes the job title, a summary of the job tasks, asjust of the essential tasks and responsibilities and a description that includes the knowledge, skills and abilities needed to perform the job.

Step two: Job evaluation is the process of judging the relative worth of jobs in an organization. The outcome of job evaluation is the development of an internal structure or hierarchial ranking of jobs. Job-based evaluation is used more often than person-based evaluation and so the former will be the focus in this case. There are three methods of job-based evaluation: The point method, ranking and classification. The job evaluation helps to ensure that pay is internally worth perceived to be fair by employees.

Step three : Pay policy identification is the process of determining whether the organization wants to lead or meet the market in compensation. The pay policy or strategy will likely influence employee attraction. Pay policies can vary across families , i.e. groups of similiar jobs, and job level of the top management feels that different areas of the organization.

Step four: Pay survey analysis is the process of analysising compensation data gathered from other employers in a survey of the relevant labor market. Gathering enternal data , e.g. base pay, bonuses , stock or share options and benefits is the essential to kep the organization's compensation externally competitive within the industry. Employee attraction can be improved by maintaining externally pay structures.

Step five: Pay structure creation is the final step, in which the internal structure (step two of job evaluation) is combined with the external market pay rates . Step four: Pay survey analysis in a simple regression to develop a market pay line. Depending on whether the organization wants to lead or meet the market, the market pay line can be adjusted top or down. To complete the pay structure , pay grades and pay ranges are developed.

In this organization's job analysis, it can infleuce these positions or job titles. For example, office support department has the lower level, front line receptionist, middle level, admin. assistant and top level, assistant to the director of operatons. Operations department has the lower level, operations trainee, operations trainess, middle level , operations analyst, top level, director of regional opertions, top level, director of regional opertions. Human resource department has the lower level, payroll assistant, the middle level, benefits counselor and benefits manager, the top level, HR director.

In this organization, the administrative assistatns, perform similiar administrative tasks across departments and do not handle function-specific tasks , e.g. HR. Thus, this organization's administrative assiatant ought be suggested grouping the front-line administrative jobs in a separate job family called office support. However, in some organizations, administrative assistant has possible to need to handle function-specific tasks, e.g. HR. Hence, in these organizations administrative assitant can be the low level group to HR department.

In the job evaluation step, this organization chooses to apply point method to evaluate the pay worth to every job title. The evaluation points method can be weights for example the four degrees for education level are identified as below:

1=high school, 2=assocaites, 3= bacholors, 4=master/graduate points are then calculated by multiplying the degree by the weights.

The compensable factor for the evaluation for front desk receiptionist as below:

skill (50%) degree(1,2,3,4) weight points

education level 1 25% 25

degree of

technical skills 1 25% 25

responsibility(30%)

scope of control 1 10% 10

impact of job 2 20% 40

degree of

problem solving 1 10% 10

task complexity 1 10% 10

120

The ensure that the pay structure is extremely competitive, a pay survey will be conducted. The market pay data must be from the relevant labor market. Surveys can include i.e. six organizations who recruit and hire similiar jobs in the regions. Base pay salary data from the responding organizations are reflected to ensure the summary job descriptions , sample data are appropriately similiar to those in this organization in order to compare and analyze the pay data between other similiar organizations and this organization.

Finally , it need to implement how to design the pay structure. it can be setted the pay ranges for each pay grade, pay ranges create upper and lower pay rates for each job in the pay scale. Each pay grade will have a minimum and maximum pay rate. It is important to remember that all jobs in a paygrade will have the same minimum and maximum pay rates. Percent guidelines below the midpoint the pay range will reach . For example, the maximum might be 10% percent above the midpoint and the minimum might be 10% below the midpoint. The percent guidelines can be based on imput from the organization's job evaluation committee, e.g. clerical and office positions: 10% above and below the midpoint. Entery to mid-level professional and management positions: 30 % above and below the midpoint.

reference

Milkovich, G., & Newman, J. (2008). Compensation,

MC Graw-Hill Irwin. 0*NET. Available at http:// online.onetcenter.org

In a highly competitive business environment organisations have to generate and sustain higher profits to survive and achieve stable growth in future years within the context of globalisation (Wolfson, 1998:5). The easiest and most practical method of generating profits is to increase the level of sales in a company. This level of sales can be increased through various methods such as implementing effective and efficient marketing strategies and focussing on satisfied customers. Attracting new customers is more difficult in comparison to retaining previous customers. It is without doubt that the attraction of new customers would require additional costs and expenses related to marketing and promotional campaigns. (reference this – if you can ask the question says who then it should be referenced)

The most important and significant strategy of retaining old customers is to keep existing customers satisfied (ref). The satisfaction level of customers is affected (would influenced be better than affected) by a number of variables such as, quality of products, prices of goods and the level and quality of service and support provided by the personnel of an organisation. This implies that if customers are satisfied they will continue buying products from an organisation, their satisfaction and the service and support provided by employees of that organisation plays an increasing role of the success of an organisation (Kuballa, 2006:10). The employees will provide excellent services and support if they are satisfied (satisfied with what?) and company management needs to keep (ensure) the workforce/sales force is consistently highly satisfied and motivated. The motivation and satisfaction of employees especially the sales force within an organisation is of high importance for them, as both the commitment of these employees in achieving the objectives of an organisation and customer satisfaction levels are dependent on the motivation and satisfaction levels of employees (Ekerman et al, 2006). (Do you need a paragraph explaining the terms satisfaction and motivation at the beginning? It may help the reader).

Many organisations regard the workforce and employees (are workforce and employees not the same?) as important assets, who are responsible for achieving the overall aims and objectives of an organisation (reference). Companies and management of companies implement various motivational techniques and strategies to increase productivity levels of employees and effectively resolve and deal with various human resource management issues (Mullins, 2005:834). Managers can motivate employees using various techniques which include excellent and competitive salary and remuneration packages, awarding bonuses and incentives, improving working conditions (including the environment), increasing the level of employee involvement in the decision making process which in turn creates a sense of empowerment on the part of an employee (reference). (deleted the) Managers in organisations can increase employee motivation levels by providing both intrinsic and extrinsic rewards to employees in different forms (Mullins, 2005:473). Money and cash rewards are one of the best motivators of employees in any context and employees can be motivated quite effectively through cash and money rewards or rewards which are materialistic or quantitative in nature (Axelsson and Bokedal,2009).

Application of different techniques of motivation in organisations is of high importance not only to ensure increased level of employee satisfaction but also to ensure increased quality of goods and services having a direct impact on the level of customer satisfaction (deleted words here) which will eventually increase the profit of a company (reference). The sales force in an organisation is one of the most important workforces elements of an organisation; they are directly responsible for increasing and maintaining the level of sales within that organisation. The techniques and strategies of motivation become more important where human resources and personnel are abundant and there is significant competition in employee recruitment and hiring (reference).

Scholars, practitioners, researchers and authors have emphasised the importance of applying effective motivational techniques over the years and argue that motivating employees is one of the most important functions of managers within an in organisations and if organisations want to succeed on a long term basis they need to consistently motivate employees and achieve high levels of employee satisfaction (reference). Providing employees with an incentive in the form of promotions, bonuses and other intrinsic and extrinsic rewards increases the level of employee motivation within an organisation (reference). The implementation of motivation techniques especially monetary based or extrinsic rewards is applicable and effective in any context whether large or small (ref). The companies operating in countries where human resource is abundant and economies are dependent on human beings such as China, India, Vietnam, Taiwan and Philippines need to implement and apply effective strategic motivational techniques in order to retain employees and attract skilled and experienced workers (ref). There are a lot number of organisations that have outsourced their operations to thee these regions due to low cost of labour and human resources but the fact remains that these regions have a very competitive human resource environment and managers in these organisations need to be both diligent and vigilant in motivating employees especially through monetary incentives and benefits (McCourt and Eldridge, 2003).

1.2 Objectives

During my job As part of my role as department manager in Toys R Us I had the opportunity to work closely with various salespersons that were paid by the company in various ways depending upon their performance and the designation they had in within the company. Some people individuals were rewarded with bonuses and incentives quite handsomely while others were never rewarded at all. This made me wonder and question whether money and monetary benefits had any significance and importance in increasing the motivational level of employees and whether or not financial remuneration impacted on the retention retaining of these employees within and the organisation.

The main objective of the (what does the refer to?? Yours or some one elses???) current research is to analyse and interpret the motivational theories and concepts especially with respect to monetary incentive techniques of motivation. The research (your research I think?) will focus on the motivational techniques and extrinsic rewards used by managers in various companies to motivate employees and increase the level of satisfaction of employees. The study will evaluate and analyse several motivation techniques and the implications of these techniques on employee satisfaction and performance within an organisation. The current scenario (what is the current scenario – do you mean in terms of your own study??? i.e. there is a paucity of literature relating to ....) of motivation is quite limited as there is a lack of research in role of money and monetary benefits as motivational forces of individuals and employees. The information and research which is present available is considered quite invalid in the current scenario (what is this current scenario???? Do you mean the focus of your study!!!!) especially motivating the sales force through monetary incentives and benefits. The research will specifically focus on the following objectives.

Studying motivation as a significant force in an organisation

Evaluating motivation as a tool for accomplishing success in an organisation

Motivational theories and their implementation in the workplace

Impact of monetary incentives in motivation and satisfaction of employees

Importance and benefits of monetary incentives in motivation of employees

1.3 Rationale for Objective

The theoretical framework of motivation and achieving employee motivation is quite comprehensive and all students who complete their studies in business management know are familiarised with the basics of employee motivation and these students further in turn go on to become managers in organisations in their professional career (ref). The knowledge of theories and techniques of motivation is not enough for achieving employee motivation within an organisation (ref). Managers need to understand the importance of motivation and realise the significance of motivation as a success factor for organisations (ref). Although managers have knowledge of the theories and techniques of motivation they fail to apply these theories in the workplace (ref). The importance and impact of monetary incentives on employees and the role of money as a motivator is taught and discussed quite significantly but managers still fail to recognise this fact (ref). Even today the most significant factor leading to shifting the movement of employees from one organisation to another organisation is the better compensation and monetary benefits. In today's competitive world and especially after the global financial crisis took toll it has become quite important for companies to retain efficient employees and one way of retaining efficient employees and attracting talented work force is to provide competitive compensation packages and motivate employees through monetary incentives (ref). Therefore this research will analyse the theoretical framework of motivation through monetary incentives and find identify how this framework can practically be implemented in the workplace.

1.4 Research Hypothesis

The current (do you need the word current?) research is carried out based on a hypothesis and data is collected and analysed from various primary and secondary sources to evaluate this hypothesis by implementing an appropriate approach to research selected for the research. The hypothesis formulated and established for the current research is that motivation is the most significant factor for the success of an organisation and employees, especially sales force, can be motivated effectively through monetary incentives.

1.5 Research Questions- is your supervisor happy with this section?

The research hypothesis described in the previous section is tested and evaluated while conclusions to the current research are arrived at by finding appropriate answers to the research questions presented here. The research questions are designed with an objective of not to be exhaustive and other information which is considered to be useful for achieving the objectives of the current research will also be incorporated into the research. The research questions are presented below.

What is the significance of motivation in organisations in the modern era?

What conceptual frameworks of motivation can be used by managers?

Which motivational techniques are mostly applied and implemented by managers in organisations?

Is employee satisfaction important for growth of an organisation and does motivation through monetary incentives impact employee satisfaction in any way?

Should various techniques of motivation be implemented in organisations by managers or is motivation through monetary incentives sufficient for achieving employee satisfaction?

1.6 Scope

The scope of the current research includes and is limited to the research methods and approaches explained in the research methodology chapter of this report. The research deals with the analysis of motivational techniques and the importance of monetary incentives for motivating a sales force within an organisation. The theoretical framework of motivation will be analysed through a comprehensive review of literature coupled with an analysis of data collected from various sources to analyse how the theoretical framework can be implemented practically within organisations. The research will specifically focus on the implementation of monetary motivational techniques to find how a sales force within an organisation can be motivated through monetary incentives. The scope of this research is limited in various ways (WHY??? Important bit) but all information which is deemed significant for achieving an effective outcome will be incorporated in the research.

1.7 Disclaimer

The current research has been performed and completed undertaken after proper authorisation and acceptance of the dissertation supervisor. The information and data has been presented in the research after sufficient assurance and consideration that all copyright and plagiarism issues have been addressed throughout the entire covered during the whole research process. Written permission was acquired from the research supervisor before contacting the respondents and participants of the research and utmost care was taken to safeguard the personal and private information of these participants and no personal information has been shared without their consent (?In accordance of the Data Protection Act???). This report is prepared in such a manner that it does not seem exhaustive to readers in any way. Even though the research study has been performed with extreme vital and important business decisions should not be made based on the research report. The research report is distributed with a sole intention of increasing human knowledge and should not by any means of trade, commerce or otherwise be redistributed, lent out, hired out or sold commercial or for business purposes with an intention of making a profit without the prior authorisation and acknowledgment of the researcher and supervisor. Do you have Toys R Us permission to do this study???

1.8 Structure of Report

The dissertation report is organised in various chapters and the layout of the report is described below.

Chapter 1: Introduction

The first chapter of the dissertation is the introduction chapter and explains the background of the current research within the context of this research. The background to context section introduces the basic concept of motivation and establishes a firm foundation for the research to be carried out. The background to context explains the context to which motivation and the theoretical framework of motivation belongs along with the significance of motivating employees through monetary incentives within an organisational context. The primary objectives of the research are also explained in this chapter to provide an overview of the research to the users of this report and what results should be expected from the result. The objectives section also explains how the researcher will accomplish these objectives during the research process. The rationale for selecting specific objectives in the current research is also explained in this chapter. The research hypothesis established for the current research is also discussed in this chapter along with the research questions supporting this hypothesis, which the researcher will try to answer during the research. The scope of the research along with the disclaimer and structure of report are also explained outlined in the last sections of this chapter.

Chapter 2: Literature Review

The literature review chapter is the second chapter of this report and provides a comprehensive and thorough review of the literature relevant to the concept and theories of motivation and the various techniques of motivation along with motivation through monetary incentives. The chapter presents a comprehensive explanation and review of literature studied for the purpose of this research and the data collected from various sources such as journals, books, periodicals, previous research studies and websites in the area of motivation and techniques of motivation. The chapter provides and overview of various theories and concepts of motivation presented by various renowned practitioners. Various models and frameworks for increasing motivation and satisfaction level of employees within an organisation are also discussed in the literature review chapter of the report. The chapter also presents various kinds of motivation including intrinsic and extrinsic motivation.

Chapter 3: Research Methodology

The third chapter of the report explains various research paradigms and approaches which, are available at the disposal of a researcher. The chapter explains qualitative and quantitative approaches to research along with their advantages and disadvantages. The various methods of collecting and analysing data are also explained in this chapter along with their advantages and disadvantages. The nature and process of collecting primary and secondary data through various sources such as interviews, group discussions and survey questionnaires are also discussed in this chapter. The research methodology chapter also explains the proposed research methodology applied in the current research and the strategy to gather and analyse data from primary and secondary sources.

Chapter 4: Findings and Observations

The findings and observations chapter is one of the most important components of a research as it presents the findings, observations and results after a comprehensive and thorough analysis of data collected from various sources. This chapter presents the interpretation and analysis of the gathered data in a systematic manner which eventually leads to effective conclusion from the research. The methods of implementing motivation techniques are analysed in this chapter with a specific focus on motivation through monetary incentives to motivate the sales force within an organisational context. The chapter evaluates the research hypothesis presented in the first chapter of the report in order to accept or reject that hypothesis while answering the research questions and eventually deriving a valid and logical conclusion to the research.

Chapter 5: Conclusions

The last chapter of the dissertation report is the conclusion chapter which presents the overall results of the research and provides the conclusions arrived at after thorough analysis of primary and secondary data and review of literature in the research. The research hypothesis which was evaluated in the findings and observations chapter is accepted or rejected in this chapter. The conclusions chapter also explains the recommendations and limitations of the current research so that any further research in this area can be carried out effectively and efficientl

Chapter 2: Literature Review

2.1 Introduction- overall you need very robust referencing here if you can say – says who? it needs to be referenced

Organisations in the current world are regarded as economic powerhouses because they contribute in the overall development of a country (ref). Organisations are getting bigger and stronger day by day and newer methodologies are incorporated by them so that they can benefit in both the short and the long run (ref). There are different terminologies that are incorporated by organisations because their core objective is to succeed in the competition. Employees are regarded as the assets of organisations and most of the forward looking organisations focus a lot on their employees (ref). Employees on the other hand coordinate with their respective organisations and in this manner a prospective relationship is created in such way that both the parties benefit in both the short and the long run. Although, employees are regarded as the assets of their respective organisations but treating these assets in a proper manner is considered as an important task (ref). Although there are different important factors and departments that are working in collaboration with each other like marketing, finance, human resource management etc but sales and marketing is considered as the most influential element of an organisation because in the longer an organisation operates and excels through sales and marketing department (ref). This paper analyses different aspects of motivation and how an organisation motivates its employees. In the similar manner the core aspects that is discussed in this research paper is that what role does monetary incentives play when a sales forces is being motivated. However, this chapter would only incorporate different theoretical concepts that are attached with the aspect of motivated and different motivational theories are discussed in detail. Referencing in this section needs a lot of attention!

2.2 Motivation – An Overview

Motivation is considered as an important factor for nearly all the organisations that are working in the corporate arena. Motivation in a broader sense is basically the activation of certain goal oriented behaviour (ref). Motivation is actually a force that forces an individual to work hard and harder in order to achieve both monetary and non-monetary rewards. This aspect is more visible in an organisational perspective where certain managers are working under the direction of directors and these managers are heading certain subordinates. The core objective in an organisational perspective revolves around efficiency of work and motivation. The employees are motivated by work allotted to them and different monetary and non-monetary rewards that are given to them in both the short and the long run. Motivation in a broader perspective is classified in two forms. These two forms are intrinsic motivation and extrinsic motivation. In a general perspective the term of motivation is used to express the motivational behaviour of humans but in a broader perspective animal behaviour is also explained through it. Motivation is associated with the aspect of incentives, enthusiasm or certain level of interest that actually causes a specific action or results in certain behaviour. Motivation is not only present in business settings it is present in nearly every aspect of life. Like If an individual is hungry then he/she is motivated by food. In the similar manner there are different related examples in this regard. Education is directly motivated by the desire of knowledge. In other words it can also be said that motivation is associated with everything that possess reward and coercion. However, it can be clearly said that the aspect of motivation is of utmost importance and it is beneficial in both the short and the long run. Specially, in a business oriented environment an organisation cannot perform well when its employees are not motivated appropriately. Motivation is directly related with the aspect of coaching and in a broader sense it can be clearly said that motivation and coaching go hand in hand with each other. The element of coaching and motivation is like teaching and education. References through out this section!!!!!!!!!!!!!!!!!!

Motivation can be explained in different aspects like motivation can be explained as the phenomenon that drives individuals to do something. Things that are done are actually linked with certain rewards or they have certain consequences. The rewards or consequences that are attached with the scenario of motivation can be of course tangible benefits such as financial rewards, appraisals etc. In the similar manner the consequences attached can be considered as the risk of losing the job etc. There are certain other benefits that are less obvious in both the short and the long run but they motivate an individual to perform certain tasks. These benefits are a pat on the back, recreational facilities in an organisation etc. (Grazier,1998) believes that believs that different members in an organisation are motivated towards the actual needs of an organisation. Grazier also emphasised on the scenario that the expectation of different rewards and benefits motivates an employee in an organisation to work hard in both the short and the long run. The researcher believes that "Each day brings with it an endless list of decisions to be made. The process of making those decisions is driven, in large part, by the hope of a benefit or the fear of a consequence" (Grazier, 1998). Referencing very very poor need more in this

2.2.1 Types of Motivation

Motivation is considered as a broader perspective and that is the reason why it has certain types. Generally, there are four types of motivation which are considered as to be achievement motivation, affiliation motivation, competence motivation, power motivation and attitude motivation. However, in a broader perspective there are two classification of motivation which is considered as intrinsic and extrinsic motivation. Both the general and broader types of motivation are explained below:

Motivation types – look at tenses below – have you lifted some text from papers etc – you need to really look at your referencing

1. Achievement Motivation

Achievement motivation is basically the drive to pursue and attain gaols. An employee that possesses achievement motivation and who actually wishesd to achieve the objectives and advance up the ladder whenever an opportunity is given. This approach is very similar to the Kaizen approach of Japanese Management.

2. Affiliation Motivation

The affiliation motivation is related with the aspect of people's drive which is on social basis. Persons with affiliation motivation perform in a better way and ultimately it results in favourable attitudes and cooperation.

3. Competence Motivation

The competence motivation is a drive that is revolved around the scenario to be good at something. It directly allows an individual to perform high quality work. When people are competent then motivated people seek job mastery and they take pride in solving different problems when they are facing different obstacles. In this form people actually learn from their experience.

4. Power Motivation

The power motivation is basically a drive which is used to influence people and change different situations. These types of individuals are more diverged in creating an impact on their organisation and that is the reason why they are willing to take risks.

5. Attitude Motivation

Attitude motivation is related with the aspect that how people think and feel. It is directly related with the element of self confidence and what is the belief of people in themselves it also incorporates the element that what is their attitude towards life and how they feel about their future.

2.2.2 Kinds of Motivation

Generally motivation is of two kinds which are named as extrinsic motivation and intrinsic motivation.

2.2.2.1 Intrinsic Motivation

The element of intrinsic motivation is considered as a major concern in today's world because this form of motivation is implemented by different organisations (ref). Intrinsic motivation is a considered as a growing area on concern because it is used to reinforce different employees and learning communities. The core ideology of intrinsic motivation has actually evolved from psychology and has been closely related with the concept of cognitive psychology (Deci and Ryan, 1985). Motivation is generally applied in the workplace and different researches depict that motivation plays a vital role in the development of leadership. According to (Deci and Ryan 1985) defined intrinsic motivation as "Intrinsic motivation is defined as the doing of an activity for its inherent satisfaction rather than for some separable consequence. When intrinsically motivated, a person is moved to act for the fun or challenge entailed rather than because of external products, pressures or reward (Deci and Ryan, 1985).

In the similar manner it can also be said that incentives as implied by the name is related with the aspect of personal qualities, intentions and values. The satisfaction that is attained from such incentives can be considered as intrinsic. These types of rewards are beneficial in both the short and the long run because they motivate an individual from insight and that is the reason why individuals who are internally motivated perform well and ultimately organisations benefit in this regard (Atkinson and Walker, 1956). However, in certain conditions intrinsic motivation might be considered as unnecessary to an individual because he/she is looking for monetary rewards. That is the reason why organizations usually try to form a complete of both these factors. . . . .

2.2.2.2 Extrinsic Motivation

These rewards are usually associated with the element of money and different monetary aspects. It can be said that extrinsic motivation is used to reduce the aspect of intrinsic motivation but this is not viable in all circumstances. Different researchers have actually emphasized on different aspects and it is depicted through research that monetary rewards definitely increase an individual's performance and different incentives urge an individual to perform more and more (DiClemente and Velasquez, 2002, cited Miller and Rollnick, 2000). In the scenario of intrinsic motivation people need time to make wide range of choices, novel events and unexpected possibilities. They need certain amount of time and freedom to make different choices in different scenarios. However, in the scenario of extrinsic rewards people are more attracted towards shortened time perspectives and that is the reason why the final result achieved is much more efficient however, it is also subject to predefined job. The element of job commitment and long term commitment of an individual may be affected negatively.

Rewards and benefits in most of the conditions are tangible and in certain conditions there are intangible rewards like appreciation, a smile of supervisor, etc. The tangible rewards are associated with extrinsic rewards and due to these rewards employees of an organisation are extrinsically motivated and through intrinsic rewards employees are intrinsically motivated.

2.3 Theories of motivation

There are different theories that are associated with the element of motivation. However, there are certain common theories that are followed by many organisation of today's world. The core theories of motivation are discussed below:

2.3.1 Taylor

Frederick Winslow Taylor used motivation a lot in his proposals and managerial models and that is the reason why they developed an idea that workers are motivated mainly by pay. His theory comprised of different aspects like workers are not satisfied with the working condition or they usually don't enjoy doing work that is the reason why they need close supervision (McClelland and Boyatzis, 1982). That is the reason why management should break down the element of production into small series of tasks. His entire theory focused on the scenario of financial rewards and he believed that workers are paid according to the number of item they produce and this phenomenon is known as time-piece-rate pay. Through these financial rewards workers can definitely enhance their production levels and they can be satisfied too. Taylor's methods are widely accepted in today's world and they are used to reduce the cost of the production system. Henry ford is considered as a first individual who utilized Taylor's models in his production lines. That is the reason why that era was considered as an era of mass production. However, different researchers believe that Taylor's approach is related with the aspect of autocratic management which is that managers take all the important decision and the subordinates follow these decisions (Emmons, 2003). However, in the longer run people disliked Taylor's approach because they were getting bored of doing repetitive jobs and they were working and characterised as human machines.

An employee can be defined as an individual who was hired by an employer to do a specific job(web.01). He has to do a specific job efficiently within a functional area or department to accomplish the goals of the firm. In most of the organizations a performance development planning process is undergone which will define the specific task of the employee as well as their expected performance. Employees trade their knowledge, skill and experience in exchange for compensation from the firm. If they are not satisfied with the compensation means the propensity to switch the company will be high, this will result in high turnover. So it's high time to give importance to the rewards.

Employees, considered as human resources of the organization are used for the benefit of the organizations, employees and the society. (Aswathappa, 2008). In order to drive the flow of business in the right direction for better results they have to be valued, respected, encouraged and appreciated .These can be done with the help of rewards. In a good working environment with efficient working methods and equipments employees will exhibit a better work performance and in addition to that natural motivation to do a job for an appropriate reward will surely pave the way for improved productivity and high profitability.

For service sector employees are the most important factor, so implementation of new reward strategies and techniques are unavoidable for high quality performance of the employees, also to reduce the high turnover rate.

2.1.1 Impact of Changes on Employees

Change is an inevitable part of life especially in the fast changing world. Today's commercial climate is compelling companies to implement changes in order to survive and grow in the global market. Changes always uproot a person and alter his lifestyle. The organizations adopt changes in order to meet the current standards; its employees also have to undergo change and should accept the new circumstances. Due to the technological, social and economic changes employees face a lot of insecurity and it's the human nature to resist those changes without knowing about its real benefits.

It's the duty of the management to handle this delicate situation in a tactful manner. One of the effective ways is to motivate and encourage the employees to put their best effort under the changing circumstances so that the net result will be high profitability and ultimate success of the business. By creating a good working environment and high morale, employees won't be negatively affected by the new changes.

In order to cope up with the commercial changes companies need to be competitive and should attract employees to the job as well as should retain the employees. Employee compensation and benefit packages are the backing up factors for many potential employees who may face discomfort in their work environment due to the social, economical and technical changes without financially jeopardizing the success of the business.

Today it's a necessary fact that irrespective of the changes which companies are undergoing they should keep their employees motivated by providing them with rewards and recognition. So by communicating the change to the employees, by making them clearly understand about its impact on organization and its benefits, the company can encourage them to do the work in an efficient manner and in exchange employees will get the rewards for their expected performance.

2.1.2 Employee Management & Engagement

Employee management is the key to effective performance management and employee engagement. Employee engagement is the psychological commitment of employees towards their job.

As said by Charles Kettering "There is a great difference between knowing and understanding". It holds true in the case of business and employees. Know your employees and make them understand about the goals to be accomplished. Understanding in business means the proper management of the employees and providing them with what they expect in return for their commitment and efficient work. Compensation can take the form of rewards, recognition, and reasonable benefits package.

The first and foremost need for the employee management is the right employee for the right job.

The keynote tip which helps to exercise a proper employee management are Structure establishment, which means that there should be a well defined structure for bringing out the desires performance from the employees such as setting of deadlines for a specific task etc. Another one is the value for employees. An organization's greatest asset are its employees so they should be motivated as well as their skills, knowledge and effort should be valued. Company should treat employees with respect by providing a positive work environment to the employees which will definitely boost their performance and to encourage them to meet the goals in an efficient manner. Listen to the employees and appreciate them for the effort they put to meet the goals and provide them ways to improve their potential, thereby creating belief that the company is taking care of them.

If the organization wants to capture great heights, all it need is an engaged workforce. It is connected to three forces in an organization – attrition, productivity and profitability. In order to reduce the attrition rate organizations should take care of the employees by incrementing their salaries, providing necessary incentives and bonus. Engaged workforce are always aware about the degree of expectation of work by the organization which yields high productivity. Thus they will result in an increase in the profitability of a concern which is the relative measure of success of a business.

2.2 Human Resource Management

The overall management process represent five basic functions for the managers to perform: planning, organizing, staffing, leading and controlling. This research focuses on one of those functions – the staffing which is the personnel management or human resource management (HRM) function. Human Resource Management is the process of acquiring, training, appraising and compensating employees and of attending to their labour relations, health and safety, and fairness concerns (Dessler, 2008pg

2).

Heathfield, (2008) defined "Human Resource Management (HRM) as the function within an organization that focuses on recruitment of, management of, and providing direction for the people who work in the organization". This can be further explained as "Human Resource Management is the organizational function that deals with issues related to people such as compensation, hiring, performance management, organization development, safety, wellness, benefits, employee motivation, communication, administration, and training"(Heathfield, 2008).

HRM is vital to the organization. It is the function which focuses its direction towards the management of people working in an organization. Dessler and Chiat (2009) states that, 'Without HRM, organizations may find themselves in different kinds of unwanted situations, such as hiring the wrong people, getting fined by government ministries for unsafe practices, finding out that people are not giving their best, or even over/under- paying their employees.'

The most valued asset of an organization is its employees because improved quality and productivity can be achieved through trained, motivated and committed employees. The function of HRM is nothing but to train, motivate and provide the employees with opportunities to be more productive and effective. Since each and every objective of business is achieved through its effective workforce, the needs of the employees should be satisfied.

2.2.1 HRM Models

HR systems and the organization structure should be managed in a way that is congruent with organizational strategy (hence the name 'matching model') (Armstrong, 2006). They further explained that there is a human resource cycle, which consists of four generic processes or functions that are performed in all organizations (Armstrong, 2006 pg 10).

1. Selection – matching available human resources to jobs.

2. Appraisal – performance management

3. Rewards – the reward system is one of the most under-utilized and mishandled managerial tools for driving organizational performance; it must reward short as well as long-term achievements, bearing in mind that 'business must perform in the present to succeed in the future.

4. Development – developing high quality employees.

2.2.2 Nature and Scope

The role of HRM has grown broader and more strategic over time. In the earliest firms "personnel" first took over hiring and firing from the supervisors, ran the payroll department, and administered benefit plans (Dessler, 2008pg 12). As technology in areas like testing and interviewing began to emerge, the personnel department began to play an expanded role in employee selection, training and promotion. Today globalization, technological and nature of work trends mean that human resource managers have taken on several new responsibilities (Dessler, 2008pg 12). Human resource management involves all management decisions and action that affect the nature of the relationship between the organization and its employees-its human resources (Armstrong, 2006).

Human Resource Management is pervasive in nature as it is present in all enterprises. Its focus is on results rather than on rules. HRM helps employees to develop their potential fully.HRM try to help employees develop their potential fully and to encourages employees to give their best to the organization. It is all about people at work, both as individuals and groups. It tries to put people on assigned jobs in order to produce good results. It helps an organization meet its goals in the future by providing for competent and well-motivated employees. It tries to build and maintain cordial relations between people working at various levels in the organization. It is a multidisciplinary activity, utilizing knowledge and inputs drawn from, for example psychology and economics.

The Human Resource Management activities extend from selection to layoff of an employee in an organization. This includes the fixation of remuneration, training, motivation and induction of employees. Thus it helps to develop other industrial relations for employees to acquire more skills and competencies (Aswathappa, 2008).The functional diagram of HRM is given in 2.2 which clearly defines the interrelation between various functions which enable the organization to achieve its objectives by providing guidance and support on all matters relating to its employees.

The scope of HRM can be limited to three aspects:

1. Personnel which mainly deals with the selection, recruitment, manpower planning, placement, promotion, training, development, remuneration, incentives, productivity, layoff and retrenchment. (web 02)

2. Welfare which is concerned with working conditions and amenities such as crèches, canteens, rest and lunch rooms, housing, transport, medical assistance, education, health and safety, recreation facilities. (web 02)

3. Industrial aspect that covers union-management relations, joint consultation, collective bargaining, grievance and disciplinary procedures,

settlement of disputes, etc. (web 02)

Web 02- http://expertscolumn.com/content/human-resource-management-nature-scope-objectives-and-function

2.2.2 Objectives of HRM

The objectives of HRM are to help the organization to reach its goals, to ensure effective utilization and maximum development of human resources, to ensure respect for human being, to identify and satisfy the needs of individual, to ensure reconciliation of individual goals with those of the organization, to achieve and maintain high morale among employees, to provide the organization with well-trained and well-motivated employees, to increase the employee's job satisfaction and self-actualization to the fullest, to develop and maintain a quality work life, to be ethically and socially responsive to the needs of society, to develop overall personality of each employee in its multidimensional aspect, to enhance employee's capabilities to perform the present job, to equip the employees with precision and clarity in transaction of business and to inculcate the sense of team spirit, team work and inter-team collaboration.

The above mentioned aims can be summarized as "the overall aim of human resource management is to ensure that the organization is able to achieve success through people" (Armstrong, 2006 pg8)

Reward is the generic term for the totality of financial and non-financial compensation or total remuneration paid to an employee in return for work or service rendered at work.

Reward, which is sometimes been refer to as compensation or remuneration, is perhaps the most important contract term in every paid-employment. Its impact on workers (or employee's) performance is in most instance greatly misinterpreted. The understanding of this term is very important; this is because the incentive scheme given to an employee will influence the behaviour and level of engagement to the organisation.

With the unique features of services provided in the First Bank Nigeria Plc, most of the employees are highly skilled and the attractive rewards they receive are dictated by the competitive labour market, which places high premium on requisite skills.

Reward strategy, in practice, is beyond the obligatory compensation or remuneration package it is a package of motivational incentives that guide actions in manipulating and controlling the behaviour of employees towards the achievement of an organisation's goal (Armstrong and Murlis 2004 sited (Stoner, Freeman and Gilbert 1995). it is in the recognition of the importance of reward as motivational technique that most organisations invest heavily in them (reward) in order to gain control of the behaviour of their employees. (Shields 2007).fracture

2.2 The Concept and Definition of Reward

According to Armstrong (2010) reward management is defined "as the strategies, policies and processes required to ensure that the value of people and the contribution they make to achieving organization, departmental and team goals is recognized and rewarded".

Armstrong and Murlis (2004 p3) defined reward management "as the process of formulating and implementation of strategies and policies that aim to reward people fairly, equitably and constantly in accordance with their value to the organization. It also deals with the design, implementation and maintain of reward processes and practices that are geared towards the improvement of organizational, team and individual performance".

Literally, according to the above definitions reward management is a motivational tools use in appreciating employees on the efforts contributed to the organisation. Which means reward could be interchanged as compensation or remuneration or explicit price of labour. Reward management is more concerned with people (employee) and the value they create in the organisation (Schneider 1987). For organisations to achieve a highly committed business environment and its overall business goal, a reward strategy must be developed to ensure that the contribution people make to achieving organisational or team goals are valued, recognised and rewarded (Armstrong 2010;p8).

2.2.1 Financial and Non-Financial

According to Byars and Rue (2005), rewards are of two types, the extrinsic reward and the intrinsic reward.

Extrinsic rewards are the tangible rewards in form of pay and benefits while intrinsic rewards are intangible rewards internalised by individual employees as a result of their participation in specified activities. Another word to extrinsic and intrinsic is Financial and Non-financial some texts also refer to them as monetary and non-monetary. The list of intrinsic and extrinsic rewards as stated by Byars and Rue (2005) also indicate the structure of rewards as follows:-

Intrinsic reward include- Achievement, feeling of accomplishment, recognition, job satisfaction, personal growth and status, job enlargement, job enrichment, team working, empowerment.

Extrinsic rewards also include formal-recognition; base wage or salary, incentive payments, fringe benefits, promotion, social relationship and work environment. This study will explain and define different type of pay and non-financial scheme use in today's organisations.

According to Torrington el at (2009), "since 1940s payment scheme have had two underlying philosophies; First is the service philosophy (experience).It imply that people become more effective as they remain in a job, so their services should rewarded through incremental pay scales. Second is "fairness philosophy" that organisations must have standard structure of reward strategy that with promote fairness". This study will describe the payment schemes which are basically in use in Nigerian.

Basic Pay- It is a straightforward payment scheme which may not provide incentives to individual workers because they are not based on output or performance. This pay is often in relation to a given period like an hourly rate, weekly wage or annual salary. It's also an established rate for all workers in one category. This type of pay scheme is mostly in use in Nigeria. Skilled, Semi-Skilled and some of unskilled labour are paid monthly but sometimes unskilled workers are paid weekly or daily

Individual Pay scheme which includes; Payment by result, it's establish a link between reward and effort, this imply that individual employee will be pay according to their contribution and output regardless of their level of experience or the post. According to Marchington & Wilkinson (2005), PBR schemes vary in practice; they can be related to the whole employee's pay or part of an overall package. Performance-related pay, this payment scheme involves paying of people according to their performance. "These are always inform of increase to basic or cash bonuses which are link to an assessment" (Torrington el al 2009).individual pay scheme is mostly in use in the manufacturing, marketing and financial sector in Nigeria.

Incentive for group, Plant/enterprise-based it is refer to as grain sharing within large group or the whole organisation. This pay scheme is use in organisations where the workforce can clearly see the results of their efforts.

First Bank Nigeria Plc, payment scheme is the basic pay which is equals for all employees in the same category. Bonus is based on a plant performance over a given period. Other banks in Nigeria mostly pay their employees base on individual performance. Along with the financial incentive reward First Bank Nigeria Plc uses non- financial incentive such as Job enrichment (giving workers more interesting, challenging and complex tasks) , Job enlargement (giving workers more tasks to do of a similar nature or complexity), Empowerment (delegation),Teamwork, Recognition, suitable working environment.

2.3 Reward System; Policies, Objectives and Condition

Reward System is an" integration of the sources and the course of actions that inform the selection of a mix of rewards aimed at facilitating the attraction and retention of employees, and to encourage employees' effort, cooperation as well as willingness to learn new skills and to adapt to change" (Torrington el al (2009) sited (Cowling and Mailer, 1998). In a simple word Armstrong (2010) defines reward system as "the interrelated processes and practices that combine to ensure that reward management is carried out effectively to the benefit of the organisation and the people who work there". This indicates that the reward strategy adapted by any organisation must fix into the Human Resources and business strategies of the organisation.

"Reward strategies direct the development and operation of reward practices and processes and also form the reward policies, which in turn affect reward practices, processes and procedures" (Armstrong 2010 p28).

Reward policies are the guidelines and course of actions formulated for successful reward system with the greatest impact on the motivation and performance of individual employees. For reward system to be effectively administered, Byar and Rue (2005) suggest that the policies should clearly indicate; The minimum and maximum levels of pay considering-The worth of the job to the organisation, ability to pay, government regulations in the labour market, other market pressures. General relationship among levels of pay between senior operating management and between operative employees and supervisors, the division of total reward into various portions, for instance base pay, Incentive programmes, benefit, Lastly, how much should go into pay increases for the next year and who should recommend how raised should be determined.

The primary aim of reward system is to reinforce the drive to improve organisational effectiveness and productivity. The productivity depends on the capability to attract, retain and motivate with financial and non-financial reward incentives people of the quality required by the enterprise (Shields 2007)

Armstrong (2010 p10) sited (Ghoshal and Bartlett, 1995) that "the overall aim of reward management should be to add value to people". In addition to this, other aims are; to support the achievement of business goals through high performance, develop and support the organisation's culture, define what is important in terms of behaviours and outcomes, reward people according to the value they create; reward people according to what the organisation values; align reward practices with employee needs; help to attract and retain the high-quality people the organisation needs and win the engagement of people.

According to a Nigerian author Atiomo (2005), the aims of reward management could be specified on three main areas – the organisation, the individual employees and collectively the union of employees

For the organisation, reward should aim at; recruiting the quantity and quality required, encourage suitable staff to be loyal and remain in the organisation, provide rewards for good performance and incentives for further improvement in performance, maintain appropriate differentials relative to values of different levels of job, the reward adopted by organisation should be flexible enough to accommodate changes in the market rate for different skills and should be cost effective.

For individual employees the reward system should be fair and equitable in valuation of the worth in comparison with others.

The third which is the union of employees, the system should ensure maximum benefits for members without undue prejudices to their future security by making their reward to pace with the cost of living and the prosperity of the organisation.

In order to meet the above listed aims and objectives, a reward system must satisfy the following pre-conditions which Byars and Rue (2005) called the desirable pre-conditions for implementing a reward for performance ,commitment and engagement;

"Trust in management- Since rewards communicate the desired goals of an organisation, the management should be consistent in relating rewards to the performance of such goals.

Absence of performance constraints-Meaning there should be no management or organisational roadblock rather the organisation should empower and strengthen the capability of employees.

Trained supervisors and managers to measure employees level of commitment and performance

Goal measurement system must be appropriate in setting achievable goal targets

Ability to pay: This indicates that the payment should be within the budget limit of the organisation, which reflects in its prosperity.

There should be a clear distinction between cost of living, seniority and merit-related rewards to avoid wrong assumption of basis for rewards by the employees

Communication of the reward system must be adequate for formal pay structure in order to be equitable and fair when compared

Flexible reward schedule must be provided especially where the pay structure is informal, in order to keep appropriate differentials with changes in the market rate worth of employees".

Considering the discussion so far, the question is: will financial reward engage employees better than non- financial reward?

According to Armstrong (2010), he suggested that "reward management is not just about financial rewards, pay and employee benefit, it also concerns non-financial rewards such as recognition, learning and development opportunities and increased job responsibility". Certainly pay is a factor that can motivate employees to work but not withstanding many people are motivated to work hard regardless of financial reward and for some, the level of monetary reward is important symbolically as recognition of worth (Marchington and Wilikinson 2005)

2.4 Motivational Theories and Rewards

The theories of motivation is been grouped by most social psychology texts into "content" theories and "Process" theories of motivation (Marchington and Wilikinson 2005)

Content theories focus on what motivates individual that is the fundamental human needs that motivate man in his environment. This theory is hinged on the pioneering work of Taylor who tagged man as an "economic man" who is lazy and must be motivated by management through pay system. His conception is that "if employees are expected to be only motivated by economic incentives, the management approach used to deal with them is to train them to behave exactly in that way" (Marchington and Wilikinson 2005).Among these category, is Maslow's hierarchy of Need and Herzberg's dual factor theory.

In the Maslow's hierarchy are five ordered needs-from physiological, safety, social esteem, to self – actualisation. Maslow suggests that the order is interpreted in a way that category of needs becomes activated only after the lower is relatively satisfied.

The dual -factor theory does not only specify the needs but improved on Maslow's theory to indicate the relationship between the needs and high job performance. The lower level need are the 'hygiene' factors which reflects the three lower level needs in Maslow's hierarchy ,while the motivators in the high level needs reflect two high level needs in the Maslow's hierarchy. The content theories establish the types of rewards which could be employed as a means to motivating individual employees for high performance.

In contrast to the content approach, process approach relates to how the knowledge of motivating factor could be applied to influence the behaviour of individual employees in a desired way. Popular among the process approach is Expectancy theory

2.4.1 Expectancy Theory

The expectancy model states, "People are motivated to work when they expect to achieve things they want from their jobs. A basic premise of the expectancy model is that employees are rational people. They think about what they have to do to be rewarded and how the rewards mean to them before they perform their jobs" (Hellriegel, Slocum and woodman 2001)

Expectancy theory is" based on the expectation that people bring with them to the work situation, and the context and way in which these expectations are satisfied" (Marchington and Wilkinson 2005 sited Vroom 1964).

The expectancy model was originated from the argument that the management of an organisation has a responsibility to both motivate its employees through daily tasks, and to produce at its most effective level.

Employee engagement is strongly tied to motivation and it can be argued that there is a direct effect of management styles employed by an organisation on the employee engagement level of the organisation.

In consideration of the management styles within organisation and how they affect the commitment of the staff to the organisation, it is also necessary to take into consideration the expectations of the staff when they enter the organisation. This premise is supported by the third & fourth assumption of the theory Y view of human behaviour according to McGregor which states:

People will exercise self direction and self control in service of objectives to which they are committed.

People have potential and under proper conditions they learn to accept and seek responsibility, they have imagination and creativity that can be applied to work.

In addition, expectancy theory implies that "management need to demonstrate to employees that their effort will be recognised and rewarded, in both financial and non-financial" (Marchington and Wilkinson 2005). The expectancy model holds that work motivation is determined by individual beliefs regarding effort-performance relationships and the desirability of various work outcomes associated with different performance levels" (Hellriegel, Slocum and woodman 2001)

2.4.2 Justifications of the Expectancy Model

Hellriegel, Slocum and woodman (2001) argued that members of staff of an organisation can enter into the work contract with a moderate level of expectancy, and an emotional connectedness to the reward they expect. However, the organization's management can and will have transformational effect on that emotional contract and influence their staff positively or negatively.

The process approach explores the psychological contract that is when a worker voluntarily makes an agreement with an employer to provide services for compensation, there is a negotiated contract. The worker agrees that his or her material or non-material compensation is of equal or more value than the time, energy and effort, he will supply to the organisation. Similarly, the organisation agrees to compensate employees in return for their resources, time, talent and energy. Therefore, the need for interviews and discussions before the signing of an employment contract cannot be overemphasized.

In order for the organisation to retain their services, (and thus reduce escape or high cost of turnover) organisation must be able to properly evaluate these emotional or psychological contracts and negotiate them successfully with the employee. Also, "management must establish schemes to reward the behaviour it want" (Marchington and Wilkinson 2005).

2.4.3 Argument against the Expectancy Theory

An implication of expectancy model is that there is such a thing as good and bad management, good management creates engagement through expectancy theory because employee's efforts will be highly recognised and target to a reward system which will motivate them to action but bad management destroys it.

The expectancy theory places a lot of importance on management style and because engagement is a function of how managers treat their staff, there are no short cut solutions; engagement depends on building relationships with the members of staff, one person at a time. Also, it is possible that the staff members are not willing to be engaged, if they believe that management are not reliable.

In addition, expectancy theory is criticised based on its focuses on three relationships

Performance outcome expectancy-this is the degree in which employee belief that performing at a particular level will attain or attach foreseeable congruence.

Valence- this is based on the value employee place on outcome deriving from behaviour or the degree to which organisation rewards satisfy employee's individual goals and needs.

Effort- performance- the likelihood perceived by individual that exerting a given amount of effort will lead to performance.

The above expectancy theory relationships explain employee's actions towards motivation and level of engagement at work. The criticism on these relationships are; some employees with deficient skills level may think no matter how they tried their maximum efforts will not be recognised, some employees also perceives that no matter how hard they work, a chance of getting a good performance is low because their boss does not like them, the reward an employee desire might not be the reward given by the management. (www.citeman.com-expectancy-theory).

2.4.4 Relevance of Expectancy Theory to this Study

The expectancy model justifies the influence of reward on employee engagement is that an employee's expectation of his/her "recognition & benefits" would directly affect that employee's level of commitment to the organisation, which is a direct measurement of an employee's engagement level to an organisation.

The expectancy theory also gives insight in the role that perception plays in choices, expectancy and preference. Therefore it can be strongly argued that employee "perception" of reward structure in an organisation can influence the levels of engagement in an organisation.

2.5 The Meaning of Employee Engagement

The concept of engagement was first described by William Kahn in 1990.He argued "that engagement occurs when a person's identity and job role exist in a dynamic relation in which a person both drives personal energies into role behaviours displays the self within the role" (Vazirani, 2010). The Institute for Employment Studies (IES, 2004), defines employee engagement as "a positive attitude held by employee towards the organisation and its values. An engaged employee is aware of business context, and works with colleagues to improve performance within the job for the benefit of the organisation. The organisation must work to nurture, maintain and grow engagement, which requires a two-way relationship between employer and employee".

Bakker et al (2008) argued that employee engagement is a unique concept that is best predicted by job resources and personal resources. "The terms job satisfaction, motivation and commitment are being replaced now in business by engagement, because the terms appeal to have more descriptive force and face validity" Reilly and Brown (2008). According to Vazirani 2010 (kahn 1990) defines engagement in terms of four components; cognitive (the role is consistent with a person's identity; emotional (the person like the role); physical (the person will work at the role); existential (the role provides personal meaning).

Most organisations presently are working on maintaining their workers sincere commitment also to increase the level of engagement because organisation with an engaged staff stand to gain a comparative advantage over their competitors. Bakker et al (2008). "Some of these interests have been generated form management observation that turnover during the early years of employment is often very high". Marchington and Wilkinson 2005 argued "that 20 percent of workers leave within the first 12 month, a further 12 per cent leave during the second year of their employment and thereafter it falls to under 5 per cent per annum"

According to Armstrong (2010), employee management is important to employer because high levels of engagement that result in behaviours such as maximizing discretionary effort ,taking initiative, wanting to develop, or aligning actions with organisation needs deliver a range of organizational benefits such as higher productivity, lower staff turnover, better attendance and improved safety.

2.6 Reward Strategy and Employee Engagement

Employee engagement is a direct/indirect derivate from employee satisfaction, organisation commitment and even productivity, some author like Bakker et al argued that employee engagement assumed to produce positive outcomes, both at the individual level (personal growth and development) as well as at the organizational level (performance quality) because employee put much effort into their work and identify with it.

Armstrong (2010) explains "that rewards given by an organisation can have an effect on their attitudes and behaviour towards their organisation". According to him, he explained that "financial incentives may increase engagement for some people in the short run, but the greatest impact on engagement is made by non-financial rewards especially when they generate intrinsic motivation through the work itself and the work environment".

According to Kyle LaMalfa (2007) he state that employer sometimes refer to reward as the labour payment for the employee's service, but for employee it is more that. It represents the recognition of their performance. Reward is a standard, which can measure how much an organisation can satisfy its staff work value and aspiration; it can satisfy their personal ideal and hope of progress; it can describe the accomplishment that the employee want to achieve in terms of position and way of living.

He concludes that when employees can feel considerate care and warmth through the fairness in reward management, they develop a sense of belonging, responsibility, obligation, recognition and loyalty to their organisation.

In 2006, the conference board published "employee engagement; a review of current research and its implications". According to this report, twelve major studies on employee engagement had been published over the prior four years by top research firms such as Gallup, IES, Tower Perrin and others Each of the studies used different definitions and, collectively, came up with 26 keys drivers of employee engagement. For example, some studies emphasized the underlying cognitive issues, others on the underlying emotional issues.

Other key findings include the fact that larger companies are more challenged to engage employees than small companies, while employee age drives a clear difference in the importance of certain drivers. For example, employee under age 44 rank "challenging environment/career growth opportunities" much higher than do older employees, who value "recognition and reward for their contributions".

CIPD (2010) highlighted "reward as a key retention factor for organisation engagement". Money is still the primary incentive used by most organisations. Reward as an independent variable showed strong and significant relation to organisation engagement. According to Shields, J (2007) "high salaries are not essential, but "good" and "fair" salaries showed strong correlation with the intention" indicating that as long as the reward is competitive but financial rewards are not the primary factor in retention.

Macey, et al (2009) support this statement that "motivation to engage follows from treating people with respect ,providing a suitable working environment which shows they are highly valued and thereby establishing a basis for them to reciprocate through their voluntary engagement".

From Macey et al (2009), they believe that pay does not motivate employee toward engagement. In addition, they stated that people may come into the organisation for money but get engaged in the process because they work for managers who are competent, have upward influence and are fair. They backup their argument by giving an example of sales people who are paid base on incentive-based that is pay base on how much they sell, they tends to " focus on the very specific behaviours necessary to get the incentive"(Macey et al,2009).

However the focus of this study will be on the impact and how reward could be used to ensure employee engagement at work. This study will consider below the work of

Macey & Schneider (2008) on engagement at work.

2.7 Macey & Schneider's tripartite concept of employee engagement

Macey and Schneider (2008), proposed a tripartite conceptualisation of employee engagement state, trait and behavioural. This state that employees' level of engagement is based on three major components;

State Engagement, which are a strong affective "emotional" component including- positive effect, energy, absorption and passion,

Trait engagement is based on the premise that individuals with similar personalities can be found in the same work setting/environment and as such employee engagement is also influenced by social climate and social learning in an organisation.

Behavioural engagement involves the influence of strategic organisational climates such as working conditions, conditions of service on an employee's engagement level in an organisation. Engagement here is defined as a set of related behaviours.

Macey &Schneider (2008) incorporated the organisation level approach to their definition of employee engagement as it is consistent with their tripartite construct, indicating traits such as positive effect, feelings of empowerment and behaviours showing organisational citizenship .According to Macey &Schneider (2008), "the antecedents of engagement are located in conditions under which people work, and the consequences are thought to be of value to organisation effectiveness".

2.7.1 Justification of Macey & Schneider's Tripartite Concept of Employee Engagement

The behavioural engagement concept of the tripartite theory of employee engagement which involves the influence of strategic organisational climates such as working conditions, conditions of service on an employee's engagement level in an organisation bears an argument that compensation policies of an organisation can have a strong influence on an employee's level of engagement in an organisation.

Contrary to Robert Hogan's view on Macey & Schneider's tripartite concept of employee engagement, Pugh & Dietz (2008) argue that Macey & Schnieder's tripartite view of employee engagement. This argument examined "affect" at the group and organisation level is strongly supported by the similarity of state engagement to the idea of collective mood or group effective tone of George (1990) ,Kelly & Barsade (2001) and Totterdell (2000).

Niven et al (2007) asserts that "groups develop collective mood because; (a) group members experience similar workplace events and thus have similar reactions; (b) emotional contagion processes lead to a convergence of mood in groups"

Pugh & Dietz (2008) also see trait engagement as a viable organisational level concept citing the attraction-selection-attrition (ASA) framework which suggests that individuals will be found in the same work setting and this argument extends to trait positive affect, proactive personality and conscientiousness.

Behavioural engagement can be seen as an organisation level concept as representative such as organisational citizenship and role expansion have been conceptualised at the group and organisation level of analysis. This argument is being supported by Erhart (2004), and other behavioural outcomes of strategic organisational climates, such as service and safety behaviours.

According to Weibo, Kaur & Jun (2010) the analysis of Macey & Schneider's tripartite theory of engagement also bears strong relationship with theories on organisation commitment by Allen & Meyer (1990).which states that there are three types of organisation commitment .Attitudinal or affective commitment (which is strongly related to trait engagement), Behavioural or continuance commitment, which is based on the recognition of the profit associated with continued participation, this at the other hand show a strong relationship with the feeling of state engagement showing involvement ,commitment and employment, Normative commitment, is a feeling of obligation to the organisation which is related to the behaviour engagement of organisation.

Employee engagement is a term strongly related to employment commitment and various author like Armstrong (2009), Reilly & Brown (2008), Bakker et al (2008) term job satisfaction, motivation and commitment are generally being replaced now in business by engagement because it appears to have more descriptive force and face validity. This implies that the word employee engagement is like an "old wine in a new bottle".

Benefit plan management procedure includes step one, deciding objective to assess what the company wants to achieve through its benefit strategy and policy, and its ability to pay for the changes; step two, obtaining view points and input from employees to collect employees' view points through employee surveys, focus groups and individual interviews; step third, analyzing competitiveness to establish or determine the company's competitive position, though conducting a customised survey or collecting available market data from external providers; steo fourth, designing the benefit package to determine the mix and sacle of the benefit package, the allocation of benefit, the scope for flexibility and the cost of benefit provision; step fifth, consulting the senior management team and employees on the proposal to get input and buy in from senior management team to make amendments if necessary, collecting comments and effort the non-financial rewards as benefits; step sixth, planning the communication to inform everyone concerned what is happening, why it is happening and how it affects them, the final step , evaluation to review the plan on a regular basis and obtain input from employees and management for evaluation purposes.

On conclusion, I feel how social changing behavior may bring negative or positive payment structure behavior to influence any organizations to decide how to make reward strategic plan indirectly.

III

The relationship between social change and human behavior

Human Behavioral network job brings social economic benefits

What does human network job mean ? Why may human network job be popular? Why human network job behavior may influence economy ?

Nowadays internet is popular to use. We can apply internet to find data , search any new things, even earn money. Why does internet

may become huma network job source. For example, e-publish may be one kind of new human network job. Any authors may apply internet

channel to help them to sell electronic or paper books from e-publisher web store. They may apply facebook, you tub etc. any online

channel to promote themselves new books to let new readers to know whether when they may buy themselves favourable new topic books to read from electronic publisher web store.

Thus, future electronic publisher industry may help any authors to build internet network platform to help them to sell and promote

ot advertise their any one new electronic or paper book topic to let global any one reader to choose to buy their any new topic books from electronic publisher web store easily and conveniently. However, it implies that electronic network platform author may be one kind of future new human network job in our societies.

How electronic network platform author job may bring economy benefit in macro economy view? A person can have few friends, contacts and still be very influential if these few

friends and contacts are themselves highly influential, e.g. one author must not need to know any one reader in global society. When they like to choose any electronic books from electronic internet network platform. They may become the author's any one topic book buyer, when they feel the author's any one topic book is fun and attract they make decision to buth the strange author whose the topic book from electronic book publisher's platform web store conventiently in short time. Although, they are strangers, they do not know themselves , but the reader can understand what it way that made Google from writing platofrm to create new creative mind and typing network job method to replace traditional hand writing book method for global authors. It will be one kind of new human network writing job.

Hence, global any one reader can apply an innovative search engine , such as google.com to find whether whom author personal new topic books are value to read from internet.

Then, the electroniuc publisher's web store may be new book store platform sale network to help the author to sell many electronic or paper books from electronic network platform

in short time. So, internet may be future new network plaform to help global any one author to create network writing job absolutely. Furthermore, internet may be popular social media

to help any one author to build goold relationship between his/her readers. It is one kind of new network, human network job. New authors do not need to buy many paper books to prepare to put in any one book shop warehouse. Their every book can print on demand to reduce out of book stock in any one book shop. They may choose to sell either electronic books or paper books both from any one book publisher web store. So, electronic network platform may be one kind of good writing channel to help human authors to create income and it can also help authors to bring new creative mind and new topic fun content books to let readers to know and buy to read from electronic publisher network platform.

Why does human behavior may be one kind of new human network job to bring global economic advantages. ALthough, it may be free income or without inocme, but the person does the network behavior, his/her behavior may be bring advantages to influence many other people's health. For this case, when a worker in a coffee shop in an airport gets a vaccination aganinst the flu, it does not only helps him or her stay healthy, but also helps the many travellers who might otherwise have been inflected if that workers caught the flu. So, the externality , the result implies the vaccination of even a part of a community conveys benefits to the whole community. For example, governments pay special attention to the vaccinations of school children, teachers, health mothers, and the elderly, categories of people particularly susceptible not only to catching, but also to transmitting a disease.

It is not accidential that governments are heavily involved with vaccination . When there are externalities, free market, fail to persuade individual incentives with society's
their the worker's decision of whether to get a vaccine ends up attracting whether other people get sick. The workers might not fully take all these other people's potential suffering into account when making her or his vaccination decision.

As Stanford University does many suggestions, understand this and tries to help them make the right decisions and so providers free flu vaccines for its staff and students.
Small pockets of unvaccinated individuals can allow a disease to gain a spread more widely well-being. For example, parent weighing the costs and benefits of a vaccine for their child is not always thinking of the consequences of that vaccination to other people. THese are markets in which subsidizing or regulating behavior can make everyone better off. Because the reason for requiring that a child be vaccinated before enrolling in school is not just to protect that child, because each child's vaccination affects others via potential contagions.

Robots take our jobs behavioral and economy influences

Robot job behavior brings economy influences

If one day robots can replace human to do simple, even complex jobs. They will bring what influences to our global societial economy.The popular economic refrain declares that the
global middle class is dying and robots will soon take our jobs, e.g. shopping center customer service jobs, library service jobs, cinema ticket sale jobs, restaurant kitchen cooker jobs,
even, bus drivers, taxi drivers etc. public transport driving jobs, accountant, doctors etc. professional jobs. Whether it is beautiful or petty matter if our future societies have many human jobs can be replaced to do from robots.

Businessman must may reduce to employ employees and reduce to pay salary or wage, when robots can be replaced to do their employees tasks. But, societies must bring unemployement rate rises , due to societies will have many people loss jobs when their employers choose to buy robots to serve their clients or do any office tasks or customer service or cleaning etc. tasks.

In micro economy view, employers may save money in long term, but in macro economy view, it will cause unemployment ratio rises , even crime rate rises when there are many people lose

jobs in societies. These models of doom, though, fail to account for the hundreds of businesses riding the waves of change in their industries when robots may be invented to replace human to do many simple , even complex tasks in our future societies.

WE may image that one small factory needs to manufacture fishes canes to sell to supermarket, the small , cheaper stuff and higher margin parts of the fishes manufacture industry. Before, this factory needs to employe many human factory workers need to help every fresh customer makeing the perfect fishing gear, designed for performance, durability, and cost in order to achieve to manufacture every fish cane in whole fished processing manufacturing stages. Every worker needs to spend about 15 to twenty minutes to finish every fish cane , till to delivery to any supermarket to sell. If this fish canes manufacturing factory can apply manufacturing robots to help them to finish any one working tasks , every robot can only spend five minutes to finish whole fresh fish cane manufacturing process. Thus, every robot can

help this factory save 10 to 15 minutes time to finsh every fish cane manufacturing process. IN fact, time is money, because when every robot can help this factory to reduce 10 to 15 minutes time to compare human worker. Then, this factory can finish about 20 fish canes in one hour if it can use robot to help it to manufacture fish canes. Otherwise, if this factory still use human workers to help it to manufacture fish canes, then it can finsh about 3 to 4 fish canes in one hour. SO, the manufacturing efficiency ensures that robots must help this fish manufacturing factory to raise fish canes number more than human workers. So, in robotic behavioral economy view, manufacturing robots must help this fish canes manufacturing factory to raise fish canes manufacturing number and deliver increasing number to supermarkets to prepare to sell every day. Robots can help this fish canes manufacturing factory bring manufacturing time saving, rising

manufacturing efficiency, improving performance and reducing wages expenditure long time advantages in micro economy view. However, manufacturing robots can also bring disadvanages to society, e.g. increasing unemployment ratio, increasing crime rate,
this factory workers will lose jobs and income, they need earn social welfare from government and increasing government finance pressure in short time, even long time in macro economic view.

Stanford University graduate program in economics, Scott lecturer explained that "in demand and supply economic theory for robots supply and demand case, robots supply number increasing may influence human workers demand number decrease. It sometimes calls " the efficient frontier".
No specific human beings were mentioned in any of economics classes. As robots supply and demand in market case, They (robots) may be purely theoretical " agents" who reached to the most reasonable sale prices in order to persuade any one businessman buyer to make manufacturing robot buying decision whether robots can help him / her to bring how much saving time , saving money, saving cost, improving performance, efficiency economic benefit before he/she plans to reduce workers number when he/she decides to apply robots to replace human workers in his/her factory or office or any service department, e.g. cinema ticket sale service, shopping center customer service, shopping center cleaning , supermarket customer service etc. service or sale tasks. When robots can replace human to do any one of these tasks in any organizations. So, robots may be human worker agents who reached to prices the way robots would react to a software
command. There was nothing that explained why some people thrived and others did n't or why truly brilliant, hardworking people could fail when much lazier folks succeeded." Having been admitted to the Stanford University graduate program in economics, Scott lecturer hoped to get his answers there.

How robots influence our future social changing? Using the right technology can be a boon to your business in this economy. For internet example, it is easier than ever to find well-matched customers all around the world, to stay in contact with them, and to more quickly design the products they want. If you focus solely on being cutting -edge, though you risk letting the technology
take over what should be very robust relationships with your customers , employees, and colleagues. IN nowaddays society, technoligical advances

and cutomation, personal

relationships in business are more crucial than ever. I mean that robots can not replace human to serve clients to let them to feel more comfortable and passion more easily. For shoe shop case example, if the shoe shop apply one robot to serve its clients to replace human shoe salesperson to serve its shoe customers. Robots ensure that they can not persuade every shoe potential buyer to make shoe buying decision more easily when robots need to contact every shoe potential buyer. The reason is simple, because robots can not touch any one shoe buyer individual emotion very easier.

If the shoe buyer needs the robots to help him/her to choose any right shoe styles when he/she can not feel himself / herself can make the most right shoe style choice decision. The robots can not replace human shoe salesperson to make shoe style choice judgement more easily. They must need longer time to analyze whether which shoe style may be the most suitable to the shoe buyer. Otherwise, human shoe salesperson may attempt to make the most right shoe style choice decision to help any one shoe buyer to chooce the most right style shoe because he/she owns shoe style sale experience, shoe style knowledge, the most important reason is that they can feel every shoe customer individual emotion to touch whether he/she will feel comfortable or happy when they attempt to help every shoe customer to seek the most right shoe style in every shoe customer whole shoe searching processing. Othwerwise, serving robots are only one machine, they can not touch or feel every shoe customer individual emotion whether he/she feel comfortable or unhappy or happy when they need to contact them in whole shoe searching processing. Hence, I believe that some tasks robots can

not repalce human staff to do very easily. Otherwise, robots may bring disadvanatges to let any one businessman to loss his/her customers, due to robots can not touch every customer

emotion to compare human staff in service tasks more easily. Robots serving customer behaviors may cause money lose and customers number lose to the shop in micro economic view.

Intellectual human economic behaviors

What does intellectual human economic behaviors mean ? I believe that when we choose or decide to do intellectual behaviors, then our societies will be influenced to bring economic growth in consequence.I shall attempt to indicate pollution case to explain how and why eithet our intellectual or foolish behaviors may bring economic growth or recession in consequence as below:

On one hand, for air pollution social case aspect example, if we only consider to buy cars to drive for working aimr or holiday leisure aim. Then, our societies air will be polluted. Our health will be influenced to bad. Our car driving behaviors may cause global environment air pollution serously. In long tiem, global air pollution will bring our bodies health to be bad. Although, ourselves car driving behaviors may bring our driving travelling leisure enjoyment and comfortable feeling in short time, also we so not need to pay public transport fare often, but we need to compensate ourselves health economic intangible loss due to air pollution , when cars number increases, dirty air will cause ouselves health to become bad.

In the result, we will need to pay more medical expenditure when we are old age, due to ourselves bodies will become bad, due to we breathe global dirty air every day, due to ourselves cars pollute air in long time, e.g. 10 to 20 years, even 30 more without limited air pollution environment. So, driving cars behavior may be one kind of human foolish behavior and our foolish behavior may bring ourselves future long time medical expenditure absolutely.

One the other hand, water pollution social aspect, if we often keep much rubblish to pollute sea, oil exploration porcessing pollute ocean , ships gas pollute ocaen, then fishes will eat polluted food and drive dirty water, due to global ocean is polluted.

In fact, because human only to conside how to buy boats to carry on leisure enjoyment activities, or catch cruises to travel on the sea. Also, oil manufacturers only consider researching anywhere to find new oil exploration places to manufacture oil product, when their oil exploration processes pollute ocarn . Consequently, global fishes drink polluted warer or eat polluted food. They will have poison. SO, human will have high chance to eat poison polluted fishes, due to fishes are poison or are polluted.

So, human is doing foolish activities, we only hope to find oil exploration places to pollute ocean or we only spend money to buy ticket to catch ships to travel anywhere in global ocean. All of these human foolish behaviors will bring pollution to global ocean. On consequently, we will need to compensate to eat polluted or dirty or poision fishes, ourselves bodies health will be bad. In long time, we need have high chance to pay medical expenditure when we are old. So, pollution case may be one good example to explain how and why human foolish behavior may influence ourselves future need to compensate serious medical loss.

All of these human foolish behavior will bring pollution to global ocean. On consequently, we will need to compensate to eat polluted or dirty or poison fished , ourselves bodies health will be bad. In long time, we will have high chance to pay medical expenditure, when we are old. So, pollution case may be one good example to explain how and why human ourselves intellectual or foolish behaviors may influence future long time economic loss or economic growth or recession in micro and micro economic view.

On another water pollution aspect hand, if we often keep rubbish to sea, oil exploration processing pollutes ocean and ships' gas pollute ocean, then fishes will eat polluted food and drink dirty water, due to fishes will eat polluted food and drink dirty sea water because the global ocean is polluted seriously.

In fact, because human only consider how to buy boats to carry on any leisure water activities, or catches cruises to travel on the sea. Also, oil manufacturers only consider any where to find oil exploratin places to manufacture oil products from ocean, when their pol exploration processes can plooute ocean. Consequently, global fishes drink polluted water or eat direty food. They will have poison. So, human will have high chance to eat poison fishes.

Otherwise, such as pollutin case, it can infuence inflation or deflation. Consequently, the reason indicates supply and demand theory. If air pollution is serious, then we will consider health issue, global cars demand number may be influenced to reduce, when global cars number demand will reduce, global car prices and supply number will need to change to fall down in order to attract or persuade global car consumers choose to make car purchase decision.

Hence, global car manufacture number and car price will be influenced to reduce, due to global air pollution issue. Consequently, deflation will occur because when the country citizen usually does not spend much extra saving money to buy car expensive goods. Money value will be low. Otherwise, if global cair pollution is not serious, human considers to buy cars to enjoy driving leisure lives. So, global car demand is influenced to increase , also global car price will also influenced to increase.

Consequently, gobal human will choose to buy cars to drive. Due to we accept to spend extra saving to buy expensive car goods. Car sale price and supply may be influenced to rise up. Money value is influenced to reduce. Inflation may be influenced, due to global car consumers number increases, we would not have extra money to spend easily. Car expensive goods expenditure influences our spending habit to avoid to make car purchase decision more easily. So, human intellectual or foolish activities may bring inflation or deflation consequency in possible indirectly in macro economic view.

On conclusion, above pollution case explain that how and why human intellectual or foolish economic behaviors may bring inflation or deflation consequency as wll as economic growth or recession consequency as well as any goods demand and supply increasing or decreasing consequency. It implies that human behavior may have indirect relationship to influence any goods demand and supply number to either increase or decrease result as well as any goods price will be influenced to increase or decrease in micro and macro economic view.

The relationship between social change and human behavior

Why does economic changes may influence human individual behavioral change? I shall attempt to indicate shopping behavior and staying at home behavior to explain their case and effect relationsip as below:

Human behavior can be influenced by economic change or economic change can be influenced by human behavior? Why does recession may influence consumers reduce shopping desire? In social recession suitation, it is possible that many people lose jobs suddenly, due to businessmen lose many customers. They need to make decision to reduce employees number in order to continue to keep businesses. Consequently, many firms (organizations) their employees may lose jobs. When they have much time, due to lose jobs, they will feel to avoid to spend too much time and money to go to shopping often. Many losing jobs people, they will often stay at homes. So, they will reduce time to go to shopping, then non essential products won't their preferable choice purchase products. Hence, recession will change many losing jobs people their shopping or consumption desires to avoid to buy non essential products often . Usually when economic boom, many people have jobs to do because consumers number must increase when many people have jobs to do. Then, many people can accept to spend money to buy non essential products often. Many people feel spend time to go to shopping can satisfy their purchase of any kinds of new products useful psychology or desire. So, recession is one good example to explain it can influence many people do not like often to leave homes to go to shopping easily. Many people like to stay at homes, becaue they feel worry about spending too much shopping time when they leave homes. Their staying home time is one good negative shopping behavior example. So, economic change may influence human individual behavior changes , they have direct cause and efect relationship in behavioral economic view.

May human behavior influence economic change? Is it possible that human behavior may bring the country social economic change in macro economic or micro behavioral economic view ? I shall indicate publishing industry example. Do you feel that if there are many students feel learning is very important when they read many books or many of students feel interesting to read or they have reading new books in habit, then it is possible that the country will have many students like to spend time to go to any book shops to choose the books, they feel that they can help they learn new knowledge. Then the country will increase students number, they often spend time to visit any one book shop every week. Their visiting book shops behavior which may become their habits. So, the country will increase students number, they often spend time to visit book shops. Also, it implies that visiting book shops behaviors may be their behavioral habits.

So, when the country has many students often spend time to visit book shops , their visiting book shops behaviors may help any one book shop to raise books sale chance. So, the country's student individual often visiting book shop behaviors, their habitual visiting book shops behaviors must may assist help any one book shop to increase books sale number absolutely.

Consequently, any one book shop , its books sale bumber must be influenced to increase to increase because the country will have many students like or feel need visit book shops habit in order to choose any suitable books to buy to read at home in order to raise themselves learning effort. When the country has many bok shops often have many students visit their book shops, then their books sale number may be influenced to increase. It explain why student individual visiting book shop behavior may help any one book shop sale number increases also.

www.ingramcontent.com/pod-product-compliance
Lightning Source LLC
Chambersburg PA
CBHW052142150726
48002CB00003B/1035